INFORMATION
TECHNOLOGY

Reader's notes

The entries in this dictionary have several features to help you understand more about the word you are looking up.

- Each entry is introduced by its headword. All the headwords in the dictionary are arranged in alphabetical order.

- Each headword is followed by a part of speech to show whether the word is used as a noun, adjective, verb or prefix.

- Each entry begins with a sentence that uses the headword as its subject.

- Words that are bold in an entry are cross references. You can look them up in this dictionary to find out more information about the topic.

- Capital letters are used to show how the short form of a word is made up.

- The sentence in italics at the end of an entry helps you to see how the headword can be used.

- Many of the entries are illustrated. The labels on the illustrations highlight all the key points of information.

- Many of the labels on the illustrations have their own entries in the dictionary and can therefore be used as cross references.

THE ILLUSTRATED DICTIONARY OF

INFORMATION TECHNOLOGY

Contributors
Zachary Cohn
Simone Lefolii

Copyright © 1995 Godfrey Cave Associates
First published 1995 in this format by
Claremont Books
42 Bloomsbury Street
London WC1B 3QJ

Series editor: Merilyn Holme
Assistant editor: Simone Lefolii

Design: Steven Hulbert
Illustrations: David Graham: Julian Baker, Mike Foster and Toni
Hickman (Maltings Partnership); Dermot O'Bryne; Oxford
Illustrators; Jeremy Pyke; Simon Tegg

Consultant: Keith Halstead MSc MBCS

Printed in Great Britain.

ISBN 1 85471 653 0

A

A Programming Language (APL)
noun

A Programming Language is a **high level language** used to work on scientific problems. It uses a special **character set**.
APL is often used in mathematics and science programming.

abort *verb*

To abort a **program** or **command** is to stop it after it has begun running. This is usually done by pressing one or two keys. Sometimes, the computer will abort automatically if there is a problem with the **software** or **hardware**.
The program aborted because the printer was not connected properly.

absolute address *noun*

An absolute address is a location in a computer's **memory**. It is a number that gives the fixed position of something in the memory. This position does not change. Where possible, software uses **relative addresses** rather than absolute addresses.
Absolute address is also called machine address.

access *verb*

1. To access is to receive information from, or send information to, another device.
In order to print a file, the computer must access a printer.
2. To access is to open, or be able to look at, a computer file. For example, a user must access a database to look at a **record**.
Access to a CD-ROM is limited to reading the information on the disk.

access time *noun*

Access time is the time taken to complete a movement, or transfer, of information. For example, the access time for **reading** from a **hard disk** includes the time taken for the **read head** to move, plus the time taken to transfer the information into **memory**.
An access time of 11 micro-seconds is fast.

accumulator *noun*

An accumulator is a **register** that can store numbers. It can also be used for arithmetic calculations. The accumulator gathers, or accumulates, the results of calculations.
The accumulator holds the result after an arithmetic operation has finished.

acknowledge character (ACK) *noun*

An acknowledge character is a **character** used when sending **data** between machines. The device receiving the data signals, or acknowledges, that it has received the data.
If the acknowledge character is received, more information can be sent.

acoustic coupler *noun*

An acoustic coupler is a device that allows data to be sent between two computers over telephone lines. It is used to change a **digital signal** into sound. An acoustic coupler has a speaker in a cup placed over the mouthpiece, and a microphone in a cup placed over the earpiece.
With an acoustic coupler it is possible to communicate with other computers.

acoustic
coupler

acronym *noun*
An acronym is a word made up of the first
letter or letters of other words. The letters
used in an acronym make a new word.
COBOL is the acronym for COmmon
Business Oriented Language. ROM is the
acronym for Read Only Memory. The
abbreviation dpi is not an acronym because
it is spoken as a list of letters, d p i.
RAM is the acronym for Random Access
Memory.

active file *noun*
An active file is a file currently being used.
The user can change the contents of the file
at any time. For example, the file being
worked on when using a **wordprocessor** is
the active file. It is usually displayed on the
visual display unit, and saved when the
user exits the program.
The active file held a list of his friends and
their addresses.

ADA *noun*
ADA is a **high level language** used for
programming. It was developed for the
United States Department of Defense. ADA
is a **programming language** suitable for
many purposes, but is usually used to solve
large problems that must respond to **input**
immediately, or in **real time**.
ADA is named after Lady Ada Lovelace, who
wrote programs more than 150 years ago.

adaptor *noun*
An adaptor is a device used to change the
relationship between two other devices.
For example an adaptor may change the
voltage of the electrical current, or it may
allow different types of **connectors** to be
used. An adaptor can also be a **circuit**
board fitted into a computer.
A gender changer is a kind of adaptor used
with a plug or socket.
adapt *verb*

A/D converter ► **analog to digital**
converter

add on *verb*
To add on is to connect another piece of
equipment to a computer. The computer is
then more powerful or can carry out a
different job.
She decided to add on an external hard
drive for more storage capacity.
add-on *noun*

address *noun*
The address is the location of information, or
data, in a computer's **memory**. The
computer gives data an address when it
stores it. A **program** can then find, or
retrieve, the data at that address.
A computer uses an address just like the
postman uses an address on a letter.

AI ► **artificial intelligence**

alert box *noun*
An alert box is a message in a **window** that
warns the user about a **command**. It asks
the user if the command should really be
carried out. Many software programs use an
alert box to remind the user to save a file
before **exiting** the program.
The alert box warned him that the file would
be deleted if the command was completed.

ALGOL *noun*
ALGOL is a **high level language** used for
programming. It was developed in the late
1950s. The letters stand for ALGOrithmic
Language.
The ALGOL language was important in the
design of Pascal and ADA.

algorithm *noun*
An algorithm is a set of instructions. The algorithm sets out the series of steps necessary to find the solution to a problem. The **programmer** must find the best way to solve the problem and then change, or convert, the algorithm into instructions in **programming language**.
Algorithms are the instructions used to solve problems.

algorithmic language *noun*
Algorithmic language is another name for **programming language**. **Algorithms** can be written in many different program languages.
COBOL, Pascal and Fortran are algorithmic languages.

allocate *verb*
To allocate is to give a job to a certain part of a computer. To run **programs**, a resource such as **memory**, or a device such as a **mouse**, is allocated.
The engineer was asked to allocate most of the computer's memory to the accounting software.

alphabet *noun*
An alphabet is the complete set of letters used to form words in a particular language. For a computer to work with the alphabet, letters are **input** using a **keyboard**. The letters are changed into **binary code** so that the computer can read them.
The Russian language uses the Cyrillic alphabet.

alphabetical order *noun*
Alphabetical order is a way of arranging a list. Words and characters are arranged in the same order as the letters of the alphabet. In ascending order, the English language alphabet starts with A and ends with Z. In descending order it runs from Z to A.
Wordprocessors can arrange lists of words into alphabetical order.

alphanumeric *adjective*
Alphanumeric describes both the letters and numbers on a computer keyboard. 'Alpha' stands for the letters of the alphabet. 'Numeric' stands for numbers, or numerals. In the English language there are 26 lower case letters, a to z, and 26 upper case letters, A to Z. There are also ten numbers, 0 to 9. Together, these characters make up an alphanumeric **character set**. The term alphanumeric is sometimes used to include punctuation and other symbols on a **keyboard**.
Most computer keyboards are alphanumeric.

alternate key *noun*
The alternate key is a key found on many computer **keyboards**. The alternate key is used in combination with other keys. It is held down while another key or a command is typed in. The alternate key is sometimes referred to as the Alt key.
The alternate key is often used in combination with a function key.

ALU ► **arithmetic logic unit**

American National Standards Institute (ANSI) *noun*
The American National Standards Institute is an organization that publishes rules, or **standards**, for the computer industry. **Programmers**, manufacturers, and users work together to agree on the standards.
The American National Standards Institute publishes standards for programming languages.

7

analog   *adjective*

Analog describes a measurement which changes smoothly from one value to another. Examples include sound, temperature and frequency. An analog **signal** is often pictured as a wave.
Analog measurements are often used in medicine and scientific testing.

analog computer   *noun*

An analog computer is a kind of computer that works with **analog** values. It makes calculations based on measurements as they are made, or in **real time**. Analog computers can be useful for controlling machinery, or changing information on a dial, chart or graph.
The use of analog computers is limited to specialized tasks.

analog signal   *noun*

An analog signal is a **signal** that is **transmitted** as a continuous wave. Analog signals change all the time. Many telephone systems transmit sound as analog signals.
An analog signal is drawn as a wave.

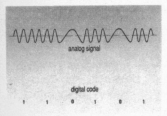

analog signal

digital code

| 1 | 1 | 0 | 1 | 0 | 1 |

analog to digital converter   *noun*

An analog to digital converter is a device that takes an **analog signal** and turns it into a **digital signal**.
An analog to digital converter is also called an A/D converter or ADC.

analyst ► systems analyst

analytical engine   *noun*

Analytical engine was the name given to a **computer** designed by Charles Babbage around 1833. It was a type of mechanical calculator. Although Babbage did not actually build his machine, many of his ideas were used over 100 years later to design the first computers.
The analytical engine used a complicated series of gears to carry out calculations.

AND   *noun*

AND is an instruction used in a **program** or **statement**. It is a logical **operation** that will give a value of true or false. The result of the operation A AND B will be true only if both A and B are true. In all other cases, the result will be false. AND is sometimes described as a Boolean operator because it uses **Boolean algebra**. This type of operation is simply performed by the hardware of a **digital computer**. True results are written as 1 and false results as 0.
Different languages use different ways of writing AND, such as A.B or A.AND.B or A AND B.

AND gate   *noun*

An AND gate is an electronic device in the **hardware** of a digital computer. It controls the flow of signals in a logical **operation**. AND gates have two or more **inputs** and one **output**. A **truth table** is used to give the output a value. The output value is true, or 1, if the value of all inputs is high. The output value is false, or 0, if the value of any of the inputs is low.
An AND gate is one type of logic gate used in a computer.

input

input

input

AND gate

animation   *noun*

Animation is used by computer **programs** to show moving pictures. Video games are the most popular use of animation. Animation is also used in educational programs and to show in simple form how very complicated things work. Artists use animation programs to prepare pictures and words that can move across a computer, television or movie screen.

Cartoons used to be drawn entirely by hand but can now be produced more quickly using computerized animation.

ANSI ► **American National Standards Institute**

antenna   (plural **antennae**)   *noun*

An antenna is a device which sends, or **transmits**, **telecommunications** signals. It also picks up, or receives, these signals. Many homes have a television antenna to receive television broadcasts. **Earth stations** and **microwave transmission** towers use an antenna to transmit and receive signals.

A satellite receiving dish is a type of antenna.

APL ► **A Programming Language**

append   *verb*

To append is to add something at the end. For example, a paragraph may be appended to the end of a page of text, or a record may be appended to the end of a file.

It is possible to append one file on the end of another.

application   *noun*

1. An application is a kind of problem to be solved, or a particular kind of activity.

Designing racing cars is an application where computers are very helpful.

2. An application is a **software program** specially designed for one kind of activity. **Wordprocessing** programs and **spreadsheet** programs are examples of applications.

A graphics program is an application that lets the user work with pictures and colours.

application oriented language   *noun*

An application oriented language is a **programming language** that is suitable for writing **applications** programs.

C and Pascal are two popular application oriented languages.

architecture   *noun*

The architecture is the design of a part of a computer or computer system. The design of computer **hardware** is known as computer architecture. The design of computer **networks** is called network architecture. Systems architecture applies to computer **systems**, and the design of **applications** is applications architecture. The architecture is important to the flow of information between all parts of a computer.

Good architecture is necessary for a computer system to work efficiently.

archive   *verb*

To archive is to store information for future use. The information can be brought back, or **retrieved**, if necessary. Archiving is different from **back up**. The archived file is removed from a computer's **memory** after being stored on a device such as a **floppy disk** or **magnetic tape**. When long-term storage is important, archived material may be kept in a separate building, or in fire-proof safes.

When the project was finished, the first job was to archive all the files and place the disks in the safe.

arithmetic logic unit (ALU)   *noun*
The arithmetic logic unit is part of the
central processing unit of a computer. It
decodes program instructions, solves
arithmetic problems and carries out tasks
which need **logic** to arrive at an answer.
ALU is short for arithmetic logic unit.

arithmetic operators   *plural noun*
Arithmetic operators are special signs used
in **programming languages** for arithmetic.
The sign + means add, – means minus,
* means multiply and / is used for divide.
*The asterisk symbol is an arithmetic
operator.*

arithmetic overflow   *noun*
An arithmetic overflow occurs when a
number has too many **digits** for the area of
memory **allocated** to store it. This may be
because the value is too high or too low. The
computer usually warns the user when an
arithmetic overflow is the result of a
calculation.
*The total ran to so many numbers, it caused
an arithmetic overflow.*

arithmetic underflow   *noun*
An arithmetic underflow occurs when a
number is too close to zero for the computer
to record. This happens when there are too
many digits in the number for the area of
memory **allocated** to store it. For
specialized calculations, even very small
numbers can be important.
*The calculation .00000000000000000031
caused an arithmetic underflow.*

array   *noun*
An array is information, or data, that is
presented as a table. Each piece of data is
addressed by the name of the array and by
one or more index numbers. In a two-
dimensional array on a graph, each element
is addressed by the array name, a **row**
number and a **column** number.
*Data is organized in an array so that it is
easy to find.*

artificial intelligence (AI)   *noun*
Artificial intelligence, or AI, is the science of
developing computers that can learn. These
computers are able to follow instructions
with great speed and accuracy. One aim of
artificial intelligence is to develop computers
that can make decisions in a similar way to
human beings. The computer would then
come up with its own instructions based on
what it had learned. Another aim is to
develop computers with the ability to
recognize shapes and patterns.
*Computers with artificial intelligence are
sometimes called fifth generation computers.*

ascending order   *noun*
Ascending order is the arrangement of a list
so that the list starts with the lowest item and
goes up to the highest. A list of numbers in
ascending order starts with the smallest
number and goes up to the largest. A list of
words in ascending order starts with those
beginning with the first letter of the alphabet.
*The opposite of ascending order is
descending order.*

ASCII code ► page 11

assembler   *noun*
An assembler is a program that reads an
assembly language program and changes
it into **machine language**. The assembly
language program is then ready to **run**.
*An assembler is sometimes called an
assembly program.*

assembly language   *noun*
An assembly language is a **low level
language** used for writing **programs**. It uses
instructions that are easy to remember, often
abbreviations or **mnemonics**. Assembly
languages are translated into **machine
language** by an **assembler**. This means
that each assembly language is generally
only used with one particular type of
computer.
*In one assembly language, MPY is the
instruction to multiply.*

ASCII code   *noun*

ASCII code is one of the codes used to represent the letters, numbers, symbols and some of the commands used by a computer. The ASCII code gives a **binary** code of eight numbers to each character or command. The binary code controls the switches that send a signal to the computer. For example, an upper case T sends the binary code 01010100.

ASCII stands for American Standard Code for Information Interchange.

Computers using ASCII code can send data to each other.

Symbol	Decimal Code	Binary Code	Symbol	Decimal Code	Binary Code	Symbol	Decimal Code	Binary Code	Symbol	Decimal Code	Binary Code	Symbol	Decimal Code	Binary Code	Symbol	Decimal Code	Binary Code
!	33	00100001	0	48	00110000	@	64	01000000	P	80	01010000	`	96	01100000	p	112	01110000
"	34	00100010	1	49	00110001	A	65	01000001	Q	81	01010001	a	97	01100001	q	113	01110001
#	35	00100011	2	50	00110010	B	66	01000010	R	82	01010010	b	98	01100010	r	114	01110010
$	36	00100100	3	51	00110011	C	67	01000011	S	83	01010011	c	99	01100011	s	115	01110011
%	37	00100101	4	52	00110100	D	68	01000100	T	84	01010100	d	100	01100100	t	116	01110100
&	38	00100110	5	53	00110101	E	69	01000101	U	85	01010101	e	101	01100101	u	117	01110101
'	39	00100111	6	54	00110110	F	70	01000110	V	86	01010110	f	102	01100110	v	118	01110110
(	40	00101000	7	55	00110111	G	71	01000111	W	87	01010111	g	103	01100111	w	119	01110111
)	41	00101001	8	56	00111000	H	72	01001000	X	88	01011000	h	104	01101000	x	120	01111000
*	42	00101010	9	57	00111001	I	73	01001001	Y	89	01011001	i	105	01101001	y	121	01111001
+	43	00101011	:	58	00111010	J	74	01001010	Z	90	01011010	j	106	01101010	z	122	01111010
,	44	00101100	;	59	00111011	K	75	01001011	[	91	01011011	k	107	01101011	{	123	01111011
-	45	00101101	<	60	00111100	L	76	01001100	\	92	01011100	l	108	01101100	|	124	01111100
.	46	00101110	=	61	00111101	M	77	01001101	]	93	01011101	m	109	01101101	}	125	01111101
/	47	00101111	>	62	00111110	N	78	01001110	^	94	01011110	n	110	01101110	~	126	01111110
			?	63	00111111	O	79	01001111	_	95	01011111	o	111	01101111			

These are the codes for most of the characters on a keyboard. The rest of the codes are for commands such as space, delete and carriage return.

= S

= 3

Each character is given a binary code. A zero leaves the switch off. A one turns the switch on.

Computers may use ASCII to send data to a printer, to other computers in a network, or to other computers over a modem.

asterisk *noun*
1. An asterisk is the * sign, or character on the **keyboard**. It is usually located above the number eight.
The asterisk is sometimes called a 'star'.
2. An asterisk, used when doing arithmetic, stands for the multiplication sign.
In the calculation 7*12, the asterisk means multiply 7 by 12.
3. An asterisk has a special meaning when used in a **search**. The asterisk stands for any group or combination of characters. It is called a **wildcard character**.
The search command *.txt asks for all files that end in .txt.

asynchronous transmission *noun*
An asynchronous transmission is a way of sending data between two machines. It sends the data character by character, or **bit** by bit. Asynchronous transmission is used for lower speed **transmissions**.
Microcomputer users can use telephone lines for asynchronous transmission.

ATM ► **automatic teller machine**

audio cassette recorder *noun*
An audio cassette recorder is a device that records sounds on **magnetic tape**. At one time this kind of recorder was popular for storing computer programs and data. The programs and data were stored on tape as sound signals. The **floppy disks** used today store more data and are more reliable.
Many games computers used to use audio cassette recorders for memory storage.

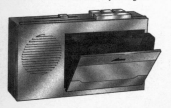

author language *noun*
An author language, or authoring language, is an **application** that allows people without **programming** skills to produce programs. The programs are usually training, or **computer assisted learning**, programs. Authoring languages generally display text and ask multiple choice questions. They can often select a **path** through the information, depending on the choices made, and record results.
The students wrote their own arithmetic quiz using an author language.

authoring system *noun*
An authoring system is the **hardware** and **software** necessary to use an **author language**. A modern authoring system can combine **graphics**, sound, **video** and **animation**. It is not necessary to have programming skills to use an authoring system.
Authoring systems are used for training people on jobs and in education.

authorization code *noun*
An authorization code is a special word or series of numbers used to start certain programs, or to **access** certain files. It can be used to keep certain information private. The user must type in the correct code. If the authorization code is not typed in correctly, the program will not begin or access will not be allowed.
An authorization code means only people who know the code can use the program or see the file.

autoanswer *noun*
Autoanswer is the method by which a computer automatically answers a telephone call. The computer answers, or receives, the call by way of a **modem**. Autoanswer is useful when no people are present, and for **multi-user** systems.
A modem fitted with autoanswer means a computer can automatically receive a telephone call from another computer.

autodialer *noun*
Autodialer is the capability of a computer to dial a telephone number automatically. The computer sends the number through a **modem**. Autodialer may be used to send data automatically at a set time, or to make placing a call over the modem easier. The user selects the telephone number from a **menu** on the **visual display unit**, and the computer dials the number.
Autodialer is useful when you send data to someone regularly.

automatic *adjective*
Automatic describes something that works by itself. A person does not need to be present, or do anything to assist in the task.
An automatic teller machine will deal with a user's request even when the bank is closed.

automatic carriage return *noun*
An automatic carriage return is a feature of **wordprocessing** and **desktop publishing** programs. The user does not have to press the return or enter key to begin a new line of text when one line is full. The **cursor** automatically moves to the beginning of the next line. On manual typewriters, typists have to return the carriage to the beginning of a line manually by pushing against a lever.
Automatic carriage return means you do not have to stop typing when you reach the end of a line.

automatic hyphenation *noun*
Automatic hyphenation describes how a computer splits a word with a hyphen without a keyboard instruction. This happens when a word is too long to fit at the end of a line of text. The word must either be split into two parts with a hyphen, or the whole word must go to the next line. Automatic hyphenation is usually set on or off with a **toggle** switch.
Automatic hyphenation is used in wordprocessing.

automatic save ► **autosave**

automatic teller machine (ATM) *noun*
Automatic teller machines are used in banks. After entering code words or numbers, a customer makes choices from a **menu** to get information or money. The bank staff do not need to help.
She checked her bank balance using the automatic teller machine.

automation *noun*
Automation describes the way in which a machine is programmed to do a job that a person might normally do. Many machines in factories and businesses use automation. They carry out a task automatically by following instructions from a computer.
Automation is often used to assist with jobs which must be repeated over and over again.
automate *verb*

autosave *noun*
Autosave is a feature of many **software** programs. It **saves** computer files without the user typing in the save **command**. Many wordprocessing and desktop publishing programs have autosave. The user can automatically save an **active file** at set times.
He set the autosave to five minutes, so that his file was saved automatically every five minutes.

auxiliary storage *noun*
Auxiliary storage, or secondary storage, is the device used to keep programs and data in the computer's **memory**. Usually these devices are **hard disks**, **floppy disks**, or **magnetic tapes**. When the user wants a particular program or file, the computer takes it from auxiliary storage and puts it into the **main memory**. The computer can then use it quickly. Another word for storage is memory.
For auxiliary storage the computer had a hard disk that could hold 120 megabytes.

babble ► **crosstalk**

back slash *noun*
A back slash is the \ character on a **keyboard**. It is used when typing certain **commands**.
The back slash is often used before the name of a directory.

back up *verb*
To back up is to copy files to another location or **storage device**. This is done in case the original files are damaged or destroyed. Some **software** programs will automatically back up files.
Students are taught to set aside time at the end of every day to back up their files.

back up *noun*
A back up is a file, or collection of files, that has been copied. The back up is usually stored on a **floppy disk** or **magnetic tape**. A file that has been accidentally deleted can be brought back, or retrieved, from a back up. Back ups also help if a file is **corrupted**.
A back up is usually copied to a storage device that can be removed from the computer.

back-end processor *noun*
A back-end processor is a **processor** that is used for a special purpose. This may be for working out arithmetic or **logic** functions, or for working with **databases**. The back-end processor is under the control of the **central processing unit**.
A computer may run faster when it has a back-end processor.

14

background printing *noun*
Background printing is printing a document while doing other work on the computer. This can be done using a program which holds the information to be printed in a special **memory** or **spooling** area.
Background printing allows the user to carry on with a new job while a file is printing.

background processing *noun*
Background processing is a computer operation which happens without the user's involvement. For example, the computer may send a fax while the user is working on a **spreadsheet**. Information is processed while the user carries out other jobs.
A computer may do several jobs at the same time using background processing.

backing store *noun*
A backing store is a **storage device** where programs and data are kept. It forms part of a computer's **memory**. The computer looks at the backing store to **retrieve** files and programs. A backing store includes **hard disks**, **floppy disks**, and **magnetic tape**.
A backing store can usually hold large amounts of data.

backspace *verb*
To backspace is to move the **cursor** in a backwards direction. There are two backspace keys on a keyboard. One is in a group of four arrow keys. It moves the cursor without changing anything. The other backspace key will delete any character the cursor backspaces over.
He backspaced over the previous word.

bad sector *noun*
A bad sector is a portion, or **sector**, of a disk that does not **read** or **write** data correctly. A few bad sectors on a hard disk will not cause problems if they are detected by the **operating system**, and not used to store data. Bad sectors on floppy disks can cause problems. Data may be lost or **corrupted**.
Special programs can fix a bad sector.

bandwidth *noun*
Bandwidth is a measurement used in communications. It is the range of frequencies which can be picked up in a **transmission**. The bandwidth is measured in **hertz** (Hz).
A wave of a certain frequency has a certain bandwidth.

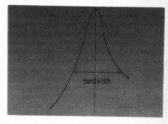

bar code ► page 16

BASIC *noun*
BASIC is a **programming language**. It was, one of the first popular programming languages because it is simple to write. BASIC is not used for complicated programs. BASIC is an **acronym** for Beginners All purpose Symbolic Instruction Code.
The first programming language she learned was BASIC.

batch file *noun*
A batch file is a group of **commands** that may be run by typing only one command.
By typing 'FMT' the batch file carried out the command to format the floppy disk.

batch processing *noun*
Batch processing is a method computers can use to **process** large amounts of information. The programs and data are gathered together in one group, or batch, before the computer carries out a job.
Batch processing is often used when many big files must be output to a printer.

bar code *noun*

A bar code is a series of black stripes of various thicknesses on a white background. Each bar code contains information about the item it is on. A **light pen** or a machine called **scanner** can read the bar code and send the data to a computer. Bar codes are often used to keep track of large quantities of items, such as products in a shop or books in a library.

Using a bar code system helps businesses keep track of inventory and sales.

This pen reads the bar code and sends the information to a computer. Some libraries use this system to keep track of which books a user has out on his or her card.

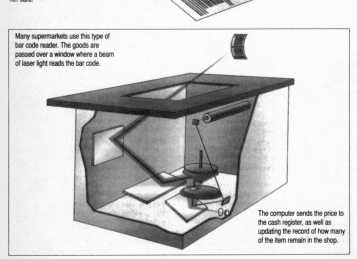

Many supermarkets use this type of bar code reader. The goods are passed over a window where a beam of laser light reads the bar code.

The computer sends the price to the cash register, as well as updating the record of how many of the item remain in the shop.

battery *noun*

A battery is a device that provides direct current electricity. Batteries are used in **microcomputers** to keep the clock and **date stamp** running while the computer is turned off.
Many portable computers run on a battery pack.

baud rate *noun*

Baud rate is the speed at which data is sent from one machine to another. Baud rate is measured in **bits per second**. A high baud rate means the data will be sent quickly. A baud rate of 2,400 baud is common for microcomputers.
The modem sending a transmission and the modem receiving it must both be set to the same baud rate.

beginning of tape marker *noun*

A beginning of tape marker is a piece of metal or other reflective material on a magnetic tape. It marks the starting point for recording.
Audio cassettes have a beginning of tape marker.

benchmark test *noun*

A benchmark test is a test run to compare pieces of equipment. It may measure the speed or accuracy of the equipment. The benchmark is a **standard** against which the results of the test are compared.
A benchmark test can be run to test the speeds of printers.

Bernoulli disk *noun*

A Bernoulli disk is a type of **storage device**. It is a flexible, magnetic disk sealed inside a hard case. Bernoulli disks can hold up to 150 **megabytes** of data. They must be used in a special **Bernoulli disk drive**. Many people use Bernoulli disks as a safe form of mass storage. The disks are very difficult to damage.
One Bernoulli disk can hold more data than the hard disk in many microcomputers.

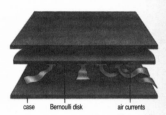

case   Bernoulli disk   air currents

Bernoulli drive *noun*

A Bernoulli drive is a type of disk drive. It uses a **Bernoulli disk** to record data. The Bernoulli drive spins the disk on a current of air. The read-write head is above the disk. When the drive stops, the disk falls gently onto the case. **Access time** using a Bernoulli drive is very fast.
A Bernoulli drive can be moved, or is transportable, from computer to computer.

bespoke *adjective*

Bespoke describes something which has been specially designed for a particular user. Bespoke **software** is software written especially for the person or company who has bought it. A bespoke **computer system** is a computer system designed for a specific use.
The superstore has bespoke software to keep its inventory records, update price lists and print reports.

17

beta test   *noun*
A beta test is the last test carried out on a
software program before it is put up for
sale. Usually, the software is given to a
number of users to test. The purpose of a
beta test is to find any problems or **bugs** in
the software before it is sold.
*The beta test found a number of problems
for people using laser printers.*

bi-   *prefix*
Bi- is a prefix used at the beginning of a
word to mean two.
A bicycle has two wheels.

bi-directional   *adjective*
Bi-directional describes something that can
move in two directions.
*A telephone cable can handle bi-directional
signals.*

bi-directional printer   *noun*
A bi-directional printer is a machine that
prints in two directions. When the print head
moves from left to right, it prints a line of
text. As the head moves back to its starting
point, it prints another line of text.
*Bi-directional printers are fast because the
print head is always printing text.*

binary code   *noun*
Binary code is a code made up of only two
numbers, 0 and 1. In **digital computers**,
data is represented as combinations of
these two numbers.
*Binary numbers can be processed quickly by
the computer.*

BIOS   *noun*
BIOS is the **acronym** for Basic Input Output
System. The BIOS is a set of instructions
that tells the computer how to function, or
transfer data and instructions. For example,
BIOS controls the disk drives, **visual
display unit**, and keyboard. BIOS is part of
the **operating system**.
*BIOS handles the input and output of a
computer system.*

bit   *noun*
A bit is the smallest unit of storage, or
memory. A bit is one **digit**, and is either an
0 or a 1. These are the two digits used in
binary code. Bit is short for BInary digiT
One byte is made up of eight bits.

bit error rate   *noun*
The bit error rate is a unit of measurement.
When data is **transmitted**, mistakes
sometimes happen. The bit error rate is a
calculation that tells the user how often an
error is made.
*The bit error rate lists how many errors were
made compared to how many were
transmitted correctly.*

bit map   *noun*
A bit map is a picture, or image, made of
dots called **pixels**. A bit map editing
program allows a picture to be changed by
adding or deleting the pixels. They are
displayed as groups of pixels. Fonts on the
visual display unit are also bit mapped.
He made a bit map of a girl reading a book.

bit rate ► baud rate

bits per inch (bpi) *noun*
Bits per inch is a unit of measurement. It measures how many **bits** fit onto an inch of a **storage device**.
The density of magnetic tape is measured in bits per inch.

bits per second (bps) *noun*
Bits per second is a unit of measurement. It measures many bits are sent. or **transmitted**, in one second. Bits per second is often used to show how fast a **modem** or other communications device runs. Bit rate is the same as **baud rate**.
A transmission speed of 110 bits per second is slow.

block *noun*
A block of information is a fixed unit of storage, or **memory**. The computer stores and moves information in blocks. A typical block size is 512 **bytes**. Block is also used to mean a **cluster** on a hard or floppy disk.
The size of a block in a computer always stays the same.

block *verb*
To block means to select part of a text in **wordprocessing**. The text can be selected by typing in a special command or by using a mouse. The block can then be deleted, moved or copied.
He used a block command to move a paragraph to another page.

board ► circuit board

Boolean algebra *noun*
Boolean algebra is a way of using mathematics in **logic**. Programmers use Boolean algebra to write **statements** that can only be true or false. Words in programs like 'and', 'or' and 'not' are part of Boolean algebra.
Boolean algebra is named after the mathematician, George Boole.

boot *verb*
To boot means to start a computer. When the computer is switched on, a program automatically runs. The program loads the **operating system** so that the computer is ready to be used.
Switching on the power will automatically boot a computer.

bpi ► bits per inch

bps ► bits per second

branch instruction *noun*
A branch instruction changes the order, or sequence, in which instructions are obeyed. Branch instructions are used in **programming**. A 'GO TO' statement is a branch instruction.
A branch instruction is also called a jump instruction.

breadboard *noun*
A breadboard is a special **circuit board** used to design new electronic **circuits**. The **components** can be plugged in and connected by hand. The circuit can be tested and adapted if necessary.
A breadboard is often used to experiment with new designs for circuits.

break *verb*
To break a process is to stop it. A computer can be stopped while running a program by pressing certain keys. Usually, the computer must be **booted** before it is used again.
On some computers, the Ctrl, Alt and Delete keys will send an instruction to break.

broadcast *verb*
To broadcast is to send, or transmit,
telecommunications signals through the
air. For example, radio and television signals
are broadcast.
*A radio station has a licence to broadcast
over a certain frequency.*

browse *verb*
To browse means to look through a lot of
information quickly. Every word is not read,
and information is not necessarily looked at
in order.
*It is interesting to browse through a
catalogue of the latest video games.*

bubble memory *noun*
Bubble memory is a very small piece of a
special material covered with a magnetic
film. When the material is magnetized, the
magnetic fields look like bubbles.
*Bubble memory can store large amounts of
data in a very small space.*

bubble-jet printer ► ink jet printer

buffer *noun*
A buffer is a temporary storage area. A
buffer will take information from one device
and hold it until another device is ready to
receive it. This is done because different
parts of a computer work at different speeds.
If **data** is typed in very fast, some characters
go into a buffer before they appear on the
screen.
*Data is stored in a buffer until the printer is
ready to receive it.*

bug *noun*
A bug is an **error** in a computer program, or
a fault in a piece of equipment. A bug in a
program may cause the program to fail or
crash. A bug may also cause wrong
information to be processed. A bug in a
piece of **hardware** will prevent it from
working properly. An engineer may be
needed to correct the bug.
*A bug in a program can cause many
problems if it is not found and corrected at
once.*

built-in clock *noun*
A built-in clock is a clock inside the
computer. It keeps the time and the date in
memory. A program can use the built-in
clock to put the time and date into a file or
display it on the screen. The built-in clock is
used to **date stamp**.
*His wordprocessing macro used the built-in
clock to put the time and date at the top of
his letters.*

bulletin board *noun*
A bulletin board is used to pass messages
and programs in electronic form. A bulletin
board is **accessed** by a **modem**. The
information may be **downloaded** to the
user's computer. Bulletin boards can only be
used by members of the same bulletin board
system.
*Bulletin boards are useful but they can also
pass on viruses to another computer.*

bundle *verb*
To bundle is to offer a group of items for sale
either more cheaply, or with something extra
included free. Some **computer systems** are
sold, or bundled, with free software. Different
software programs are sometimes bundled
and sold together at a cheaper price than
the cost of buying them all as separate
items.
*The mail order company decided to bundle a
database and a wordprocessing program
with an expansion card.*
bundle *noun*

ureau *noun*

 bureau is an office that does computer
'ork. It may offer **wordprocessing** or
esktop publishing services. A bureau
ay also offer other services, such as **fax**
ansmission or telephone answering. For
'ork using colour graphics, or for a large
ailing, a bureau can be very useful.
*he artist took her graphics file to a bureau
ecause they had a very good colour printer.*

urst mode *noun*

urst mode is a way in which data can be
ansferred. Data is sent very quickly
etween the **central processing unit** and a
eripheral device in one group, or burst.
urst mode is a quick way to transfer data.

us *noun*

 A bus is a kind of **network**. The
omputers in the network are all connected
y one long **cable**.
he bus is used to link many area networks.

 The bus is the channel, or **path**, which
ts the parts of a computer communicate
ith each other. There are different types of
us. An expansion bus allows more
ardware to be attached to the system. An
O bus handles input and output signals.
he bus provides the **circuits** for an
xpansion slot. There are 8-bit and 16-bit
uses.
*bus is like a road along which signals are
ent.*

business graphics *plural noun*

Business graphics are images and pictures
usually combined with text. They are created
to show information simply and clearly.
Business graphics often include charts and
graphs. The software usually makes it easy
to **import** text or numbers from other
software packages.
*Business graphics can make a presentation
far more interesting.*

button *noun*

A button is a word or **icon** that a person can
click a mouse on, causing a command to be
carried out. For example, clicking on a
button can start another program running.
*The menu presented him with a choice of six
buttons.*

byte ► page 22

byte *noun*

A byte is a unit of measure of computer **memory**. One byte is usually made up of eight **bits**. Every character or symbol entered into the computer takes up one byte of memory. Each byte is stored in a **cell** at a particular **address**. There are a thousand bits in a kilobyte, a thousand kilobytes in a megabyte, and a thousand megabytes in a gigabyte.

Most computers have millions of bytes of memory.

When the letter 'b' is entered, the binary code 01100010 is sent to RAM. Each circuit, or switch, is one bit. All eight together equal one byte.

1 byte = 1 character

1 Kbyte =
1,000 bytes =
1,024 characters
or half a page

1 Mbyte = 1,000 Kbyte
= 1,048,576 characters
or 500 pages

1 Gbyte = 1,000 Mbyte
= 1,073,741,824 or 500,000,000 page

C

C (language) *noun*
C is a popular **programming language**. It is used for writing **systems software** and **applications**. C is a **high level language** but can make use of **low level** instructions.
C is more difficult to learn than BASIC or FORTRAN.

cable *noun*
A cable is a length of wire or wires inside a protective covering. Cables are used to connect parts of a computer, and to connect systems on a **network**. Most cables used in computing and **telecommunications** are **fibre optic** or **coaxial cables**. The correct cable must be used for a particular job. Cables come with a variety of **connectors**.
A printer cable must have the right connectors or it will not plug into the port.

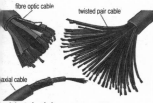

fibre optic cable

twisted pair cable

coaxial cable

cable television ► page 24

cable network *noun*
A cable network is a **cable television** station. It also includes the television sets connected to the network.
Users pay to join a cable network.

cache *noun*
A cache is an area in a computer's **memory** used for temporary storage of information. It stores information that is being used, or was recently **retrieved**. The **active file** is often put into the cache. It is quicker for the computer to **access** information from the cache than from a disk.
The cache speeds up the operation of a computer.

cache memory *noun*
Cache memory is high speed **memory**. It can store less than the normal memory of the computer, but speeds up the system by providing a **cache**.
Extra cache memory was added to a computer.

CAD *noun*
CAD is the **acronym** for Computer Aided Design. CAD programs are used to design objects and to produce technical drawings. For example, CAD is used to design houses, aeroplanes or machine parts. The computer carries out many of the calculations.
Many architects use CAD to help them design buildings.

CAD/CAM ► page 26

CAI ► **computer aided instruction**

calculation *noun*
A calculation is used in mathematics. To find the answer to a problem a calculation is done using addition, subtraction, multiplication or division.
Many computers can carry out millions of calculations in one second.

call *noun*
A call is a **statement** that tells a computer **program** to obey a **subroutine**. When the subroutine has been completed, the program goes back to the instruction following the call statement.
The subroutine was entered using call.

cable television   *noun*

Cable television is a television service delivered by **cable**. A station called a headend receives signals from satellites and other television stations. It may also produce its own television programmes. Cable television allows two-way signals, so people can send information back to the headend. Shopping, banking, and **electronic mail** are some of the uses being developed.

There is usually a fee for receiving cable television broadcasts.

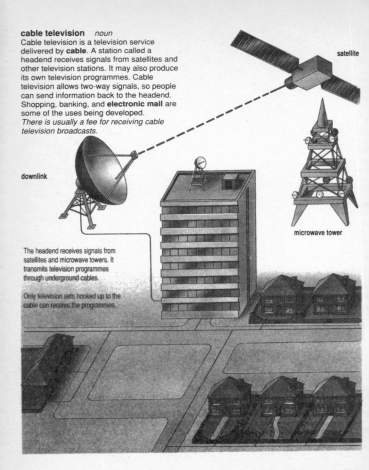

satellite

microwave tower

downlink

The headend receives signals from satellites and microwave towers. It transmits television programmes through underground cables.

Only television sets hooked up to the cable can receive the programmes.

CALL *noun*

CALL is the **acronym** for Computer Assisted Language Learning. It is used to describe computer programs which help a student learn a foreign language. CALL programs are often used together with cassettes and videos.

Part of her CALL program was typing the word she heard into the computer in Spanish.

call forwarding *noun*

Call forwarding is a service offered by some telephone companies. The user can ask for their telephone calls to be automatically forwarded to a different number.

Call forwarding is useful to people who travel as part of their work.

CAM *noun*

CAM is the **acronym** for Computer Aided Manufacture. CAM is used to control machines making products in factories. CAM also keeps track of other things needed to make the product. For example, it may store information on the materials, accounting and labour. A good CAM system will save a manufacturer time and money.

Machine tools are controlled by CAM in many modern factories.

cancel command *noun*

The cancel command is used when the user changes their mind. The computer returns to the previous command or display.

She sent a cancel command because she decided not to print the document.

capacity *noun*

Capacity is the amount of information a **storage device** can hold. Capacity is measured in **bytes**.

A 20-megabyte hard disk has the capacity to hold twenty million bytes of data.

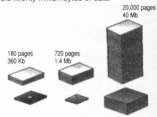

20,000 pages
40 Mb

180 pages
360 Kb

720 pages
1.4 Mb

caps lock *noun*

The caps lock is a key on a computer's **keyboard**. When it is pressed, all the letters typed will be in capitals, or upper case. When caps lock is pressed again, the keyboard returns to normal. The caps lock key is a **toggle switch**.

He pressed the caps lock and then typed HOW ARE YOU?

card *noun*

A card is a **circuit board** that fits into the computer. The card lets the user add new features to the computer. These might include colour, **video** or a **modem**.

The engineer fitted the new video card in the second expansion slot.

carriage return *noun*

The carriage return is a key on a keyboard. When it is pressed, the **cursor** moves down a line. A command is also stored to tell a printer to move the print head down a line. A carriage return is usually used to separate paragraphs in a **wordprocessing** document. Sometimes the carriage return key has the word 'return' or 'enter' on it.

Pressing the carriage return twice will leave a blank line on the page.

CAD/CAM *noun*

CAD/CAM is the **acronym** for Computer
Aided Design and Computer Aided
Manufacture. CAD/CAM is a **system** of
using computers to design and make a
product. CAD/CAM is often used in
mechanical engineering.
*The engineer designed and made a special
nut and bolt using CAD/CAM.*

typical workstation

user
manuals

mouse

puck

digitizing
tablet

tape
back up

file server

print server

plotter

machine tool

carrier signal *noun*
A carrier signal is a **signal** that is added to a second signal. Two signals are usually sent in a communications **transmission**. The data signal contains information, or a message. The carrier signal is added to the data signal. This changes the signal so that it is more regular. It is this combination of signals that travels down a transmission line.
A carrier signal has a regular wave pattern.

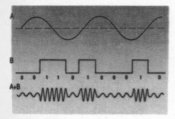

A   carrier signal
B   data signal
A+B modulated signal

cartridge *noun*
A cartridge is a protective case or covering. It may be used to hold a disk, **magnetic tape**, a printer ribbon or **toner**. The contents are sealed inside a plastic container so that they cannot be damaged.
Audio tapes come sealed inside a cartridge.

case sensitive *noun*
Case sensitive means that the computer will not recognize one letter of the alphabet as the same letter in both **lower case** and **upper case**. For example, it will not recognize the letter G as being the same letter as g. In some programs, it is important whether or not data is typed using upper case or lower case letters.
She set the computer to case sensitive in order to find the word GIGABYTE only where it appeared in upper case letters.

cathode ray tube (CRT) *noun*
A cathode ray tube is the biggest part of most **visual display units** and television sets. The screen is the front of the cathode ray tube. The cathode ray tube sends an electron beam backwards and forwards very quickly over the screen. When the beam strikes the phosphor coating on the inside of the screen, a picture is formed.
Cathode ray tubes are too big to be used on portable computers.

CBT ► **computer based training**

CCD ► **charge coupled device**

CD ► **compact disk**

CDI ► **compact disk interactive**

CD-ROM *noun*
CD-ROM is the **acronym** for Compact Disk Read Only Memory. It is a **compact disk** which is used to store data. The user can only **read** a CD-ROM, not add to it. Some CD-ROM's hold up to 250,000 pages of information on one disk.
CD-ROMs are a type of optical disk storage.

cell *noun*
1. A cell is a location on a **spreadsheet**. It is a box which can hold information. A cell can have a number, text or a formula in it.
A cell is found using a column number and a row number.
2. A cell is an area in memory that stores one unit of information.
Each cell is given its own address.

cellular telephone *noun*
Cellular telephone is a mobile telephone
service. Telephone calls are **transmitted**
through the air. If necessary, a call can be
sent to a local telephone exchange and sent
over telephone lines. An automatic switching
system lets the user move from one area, or
cell, to another during a telephone call.
Cellular telephones are portable.

central processing unit (CPU) *noun*
The central processing unit is the main part
of a computer. It carries out all of the
instructions from a program. The central
processing unit contains the **arithmetic
logic unit**, the control unit, the **registers**
and often some **memory**.
*The central processing unit is sometimes
called the central processor or processor.*

Centronics interface *noun*
The Centronics interface is a **standard** for
connecting printers to a computer. It is a
parallel interface. Most microcomputers
have a Centronics **port**. A Centronics **cable**
connects the two devices.
*It is simple to connect a computer and a
printer manufactured by different companies
if they both use a Centronics interface.*

CGA ▶ colour graphics adaptor

chain *verb*
To chain is to link together information. The
information can then be **searched** quickly.
*Some programming languages allow
information to be chained.*

channel *noun*
A channel is a path between two machines,
or devices. Users at each end are able to
communicate with each other. In computers,
the channel may only be in one direction,
such as information sent to a printer.
*Telephone wires provide channels between
the person who is calling and the person
who answers.*

character *noun*
A character is any **digit**, letter, punctuation
mark or symbol. A character is usually
stored in one **byte** in a computer. For the
computer, B and b are different characters.
If the letter B is printed in bold, it is still said
to be the same character but with different
attributes.
*Each number and letter on a keyboard is a
character.*

character code *noun*
The character code is a code that gives
each **character** a number. It is the character
codes which are stored in a computer's
memory, and which cause the character to
appear when sent to a printer or to the
screen. **ASCII code** and **EBCDIC** are two
examples of character codes.
*Most character codes use the binary digits 0
and 1.*

character set *noun*
A character set is the group of characters
that appear on a computer **keyboard**.
A character set includes characters that print
and also characters that cannot be seen.
These are, for example, the delete key,
backspace key and space bar.
ASCII code covers a complete character set.

characters per inch (CPI) *noun*
Characters per inch is a measurement of the
number of characters a printer prints in one
inch. It is also used to describe the length of
words in a particular **font**.
*The printer could print a choice of 10 or 12
characters per inch.*

29

characters per second (CPS) *noun*
Characters per second is a measurement of how fast a printer can print. Different printers print at different speeds. The speed is measured by how many characters the printer prints in one second.
Many dot matrix printers can print more than 200 characters per second.

charge coupled device (CCD) *noun*
A charge coupled device is a type of **memory**. It uses electronic **components** that can be charged, or powered, by light or electricity. A computer or **microprocessor** can read the pattern of the charges. Many **scanners** use a charge coupled device to record how dark or light each **pixel** is on the document being **scanned**.
Scientists are working on improving charge coupled devices for use as computer memory.

chassis *noun*
The chassis is the case, or framework, that holds a machine. The chassis of a computer holds the **central processing unit**, any **expansion cards**, and the **disk drive**.
The motherboard usually sits on the bottom of a computer's chassis.

chip ► silicon chip

circuit *noun*
A circuit is a number of electronic **components** joined together to form a path for electricity. The components may be on a **printed circuit board** or on a **silicon chip**.
A closed circuit will allow electric current to flow.

circuit board *noun*
A circuit board is a flat plastic plate with thin copper strips. These strips connect different electronic **components** mounted on the board, including **integrated circuits**. An **edge connector** is usually used to join a circuit board to the rest of a machine.
Circuit boards are used in many electronic machines.

CISC *noun*
CISC is short for Complex Instruction Set Computer. A CISC is a type of **processor**. It can carry out a great number of instructions very quickly. Most computers are CISC computers, although a growing number use a **RISC** processor.
All of the computers in the school are CISC computers.

click *verb*
To click means to press and release a button on the **mouse**. Clicking sends a command to the computer. A joystick also has a button on the top which can be clicked.
The instructions said to click on the picture of two dice to start the game.

clip art *noun*
Clip art is pictures that are supplied ready to use. Clip art is often used in **desktop publishing**. The pictures, or images, can be stored in the computer. A piece of clip art can be put anywhere on a page, made bigger or smaller, or turned upside down.
He opened his clip art file and put a picture of a horse onto the page.

clock speed *noun*
Clock speed is a measurement of how fast a **microprocessor** runs. The unit of measurement is **megahertz**. Clock speed is used to compare the speeds of different computers, although the **architecture**, **storage devices** and **software** are also important.
The higher the clock speed, the faster a computer will operate.

clone *noun*
A clone is a copy, or duplicate, of something.
Many computer manufacturers have
produced clones of the IBM personal
computer. A clone should be **compatible**
with the original device.
*A clone can run the same software as the
original model without making any changes.*
clone *verb*

close *verb*
To close means to stop using a **file** or an
application. When the user chooses the
close command, the program and the files in
use are shut down. The computer can then
carry out another task.
*She finished typing her letter, so she closed
the wordprocessing application by choosing
'Close' from the menu.*

cluster *noun*
1. A cluster is a group of computers or
devices that are near each other. They often
share a printer and other **peripherals** such
as a **tape streamer**.
*There is a cluster of computers in the data
processing department.*
2. A cluster is an area on a disk. Data is
stored in clusters on a **hard disk** or a **floppy
disk**. Parts of a file might be put in different
clusters on the disk. Another word for cluster
is block.
*Each cluster is in one track and within one
sector of a disk.*

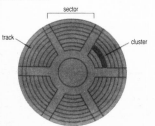

CMOS *noun*
CMOS is the **acronym** for Complementary
Metal Oxide Semiconducior. It describes a
type of **integrated circuit** made of a special
material. The semiconductor is made in
layers of positive and negative material.
*CMOS circuits do not use much power so
they are ideal for portable computers.*

CMYK *noun*
CMYK stands for the four colours used when
printing in colour. C stands for cyan, a kind
of blue. M stands for magenta, a kind of red.
Y stands for yellow and K stands for key,
which is black. All colours can be printed
using a mixture of these colours.
*Some desktop publishing packages use
CMYK so that a printing company can print
directly from a floppy disk.*

coaxial cable *noun*
Coaxial cable is a type of **cable** used in
telecommunications. It consists of an inner
wire or wires and an outer tube, separated
by insulation. The outside is covered with a
protective layer. Data is sent through coaxial
cables.
*Coaxial cables may be used to connect
computers in a network or a television
antenna to a television set.*

COBOL *noun*
COBOL is the acronym for Common
Business Oriented Language. It is a **high-
level language** used for **programming**.
COBOL is easy to learn and read. It is used
on **mainframe** computers.
*COBOL is used for many business
applications.*

code ► **character code; machine
code**

code *noun*
A code is a way of using signs and symbols to represent letters or whole words. Most computers work using **binary code**. Binary code uses a sequence of numbers to stand for the letters, numbers and symbols of ordinary language.
ASCII is a code used by many types of computer.

colour graphics adaptor (CGA) *noun*
The colour graphics adaptor is a **standard** for **visual display units**. It can display four colours at a **resolution** of 320 by 200 **pixels** in graphics mode. In text mode it allows one colour to be displayed at a resolution of 640 by 200 pixels.
She fitted the colour graphics adaptor in the expansion slot.

column *noun*
A column is information set out in a narrow strip down a page. A column may be given a number, letter or name so that it can be referred to easily. Columns are used in **spreadsheets** and in **desktop publishing**.
The column was labelled 'Hours Worked'.

COM *noun*
COM is the **acronym** of Computer Output on Microfilm. A computer sends, or outputs, information to a special machine that records it on **microfilm**. The information is printed in very small letters, and is read using a machine that magnifies the text.
COM uses less space to store information than documents on paper.

command *noun*
A command is an instruction to a computer or other device. The computer must be able to recognize the command. A user can type in each command separately, or use a **menu** to choose a command from an existing list.
The exit command will close a software program.
command *verb*

command-driven *adjective*
Command-driven describes a software program that lets a user type in **commands**. The other way to give commands is by using **menus** or **icons**.
A command-driven program waits for the user to type in a command.

command line interpreter *noun*
The command line interpreter is the part of the **operating system** that receives and obeys commands typed by the user.
A command line interpreter is needed for a command-driven software program.

comment *noun*
A comment is used in **programming**. It is a message that reminds the programmer, or tells a new programmer, what a set of instructions means. A comment does not change what happens when the program is run. Comments are also used in files. They do not print when the file is printed.
The comment said 'This line puts a square shape in the middle of the visual display unit'.

communications *noun*
The transferring of information is called communications. People communicate by speaking or writing to each other. Machines communicate by sending information through cables, or by sending signals through the air.
Communications play an important role in the world of business.
communicate *verb*

communications link *noun*
A communications link is the **path** systems use to transfer information.
A communications link can be made through cables or by signals sent over the air.

communications system *noun*
A communications system is all the equipment which must be connected together in order to send and receive information. Computers connected by **networks** are an example of a communications system. Telephones use a telephone communications system.
Communications systems play an important part in gathering world news.

compact disk *noun*
A compact disk is a plastic disk used to store information. It is used for music and for computer data. Compact disks are **optical disks**. They use light to read data.
A compact disk is made up of many layers.

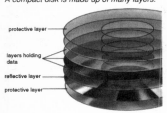

protective layer —
layers holding data —
reflective layer —
protective layer —

compact disk interactive (CDI) *noun*
Compact disk interactive is a set of rules, or a **standard**, created especially so that **compact disks** can be used to store information. It allows a compact disk player to use a television to display information. Compact disks following the standard, which allow the user make choices about how to move through the information on the disk. This is why it is called **interactive**.
Compact disk interactive is used with a special keypad and a television set.

compact disk read only memory ►
CD-ROM

compatible *adjective*
Compatible describes **hardware** or **software** that can work with different computers.
A printer made by one company is compatible if it works with a computer made by a different company.

complementary metal oxide semiconductor ► CMOS

complex instruction set computer ►
CISC

compiler *noun*
A compiler is a **program** that changes a **programming language** into **machine code**.
High level languages cannot be run without first going through a compiler.

component *noun*
1. A component is one piece of equipment. A printer is a component. So is a **keyboard**. All the components, or pieces of hardware, that work together are called a **system**.
An external hard drive is a component of some computer systems.
2. A component is an electronic device. A group of components are fixed to a **printed circuit board** inside electronic machines.
There are many different types of component, each carrying out a special job.

33

computer ► page 36

computer aided design ► **CAD**

computer aided instruction (CAI)
noun
Computer aided instruction is a term used to describe programs used in schools and for training. Students use computer aided instruction to help them learn. The programs are often **interactive** and combine video, sound and animation with text.
Computer aided instruction uses computer programs to teach a subject.

computer aided manufacture ► **CAM**

computer based training (CBT) *noun*
Computer based training uses computers to teach people how to do a job. It is similar to **computer aided instruction** but is usually used to describe programs that train people to carry out a particular task.
Computer based training can be used to teach someone a new software program.

computer game *noun*
A computer game is an **electronic** game. It is played in an arcade, on a **microcomputer**, or on a handheld device. Computer games are **interactive**.
She entered a competition to write a computer game in one day.

computer graphics ► **graphics**

computer literate *adjective*
Computer literate means that a person is able to use a computer. The person knows enough about **software** and **hardware** in order to run **programs**. A computer literate person can **input** data into a machine and get **output** from it.
By the time the course finished, the students were computer literate.

computer output on microfilm ► **COM**

computer system *noun*
A computer system is all of the **hardware** and **software** that works together with the computer. A computer system can be a **microcomputer** or a large **mainframe**. *Peripherals such as a keyboard, printer or floppy disk are all part of the computer system.*

concatenate *verb*
To concatenate means to put things together. In **programming**, two **strings** are concatenated to form a new string. The string 'comp' is concatenated to the string 'uter' to form the string 'computer'.
He set the photocopy machine to concatenate six copies of the report.

concurrent processing ► **multitasking**

conductor *noun*
A conductor is a material that allows electricity or heat to pass through it easily. In **telecommunications**, copper is the material normally used as a conductor.
Copper wire is used as the conductor in coaxial cable.

configuration *noun*
A configuration is an arrangement. It is how all of the hardware and software in a **computer system** is organized so that each part works correctly.
The engineer checked the printer configuration.

configure *verb*
1. To configure is to put together hardware and software for a **computer system**. A system to produce graphics would probably be configured with a large **storage device** and a colour **visual display unit**.
The computer company was asked to configure a system for the zoo.
2. To configure is to set up software in a special way. The user can choose different options so that the program will be easier to use. To configure a wordprocessing program, for example, the user can choose what font will be displayed, the colour of the letters, and the size of the page when the program begins.
She decided to configure the computer so that the screen displayed blue letters on a grey background.
configuration *noun*

connectivity *noun*
Connectivity is a measure of how easy it is to connect devices together.
Connectivity is an important part of being user friendly.

connector *noun*
A connector is a fitting used to connect or separate two electrical devices.
The machines used in information technology have many different types of connector.

console *noun*
A console is the **visual display unit** and the **keyboard** of a computer.
There were six consoles in the travel agency.

constant *noun*
A constant is a value that does not change. It is used in **programming**. The constant may have a name to make the program easier to read.
A constant with the name TAX might be given the value 17.5.

continuous paper *noun*
Continuous paper is paper that goes through a printer in a continuous length. The paper usually has holes, called sprocket holes, along the edges. Continuous paper is fed into the printer automatically. It can be cut easily along special lines, or perforations.
The accountant used continuous paper to print 10,000 invoices.

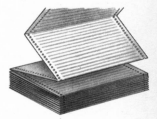

contrast control *noun*
The contrast control is a knob that makes information on the **visual display unit** lighter or darker. It is used to make the display easier to read. For example it can increase or reduce the difference between the characters and the screen colour.
The contrast control is usually at the back of the visual display unit or on the side of it.

control character *noun*
A control character is a character used to give special instructions. A control character is not seen by the user. For example, the delete key on a keyboard sends a control character to the computer.
A control character is used to tell a modem that a message has ended.

computer *noun*

A computer is a machine that can store information and change, or **process** it. It does this by following the instructions of a **program**. Today, computers are electronic. Depending on how powerful they are, computers are classed as **microcomputers**, **minicomputers**, **mainframe** computers or **supercomputers**.
Most computers are digital computers.

Early computers used mechanical devices for memory and calculation. The Jacquard loom used punched cards.

size in relation to a pencil point

vacuum tube

The first electronic computers used vacuum tubes. They were very large, quite slow, and not very reliable. Thousands of vacuum tubes were used. These computers are sometimes called first generation computers.

size in relation to a pencil point

transistor

When transistors were invented, the size of computers was reduced and the speed was increased. Hundreds of transistors were used. This made the computers much more reliable. Transistorized computers are called second generation computers.

size in relation to a pencil point

integrated circuit

The invention of the integrated circuit meant that computers became much more powerful and much smaller. One tiny integrated circuit is equivalent to thousands of transistors. These are known as third generation computers.
More and more circuits were put onto a single chip. Today's fourth generation computers are still getting smaller, and more powerful.

Charles Babbage's analytical engine used a series of interlocking gears.

Mechanical adding machines were eventually replaced by electronic ones.

These computers filled many rooms.

These computers can make 5,000 additions, or 300 multiplications per second.

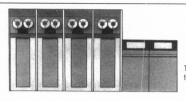

These computers filled a large room.

These computers can make 1,000,000 calculations per second.

These computers sit on a desktop, or can be small enough to fit in a pocket.

These computers can make tens of millions of calculations per second.

control key *noun*
The control key is a key on a computer **keyboard**. It is used with other keys to send **commands** or produce special characters on the visual display unit.
The control key is held down while another key or keys are pressed.

control unit *noun*
The control unit is the part of the **central processing unit** that sends instructions in the correct order. It fetches instructions from the computer's memory and gets them ready for the **processor**. After processing, the control unit puts the result back into the **memory**. The control unit also keeps track of data being copied onto a disk.
The control unit is sometimes called the controller.

conversion program *noun*
A conversion program is a **program** that changes, or converts, another program so that it can run on a different computer. A conversion program may also be used to change the characters in a file from one **character code** to another.
She used a conversion program so that she could work with a file from another computer.

coprocessor *noun*
A coprocessor is an additional **processor** that helps a **computer system** run faster. It takes some of the work from the **central processing unit**.
After he installed the math coprocessor, the answers appeared more quickly on the visual display unit.

copy *verb*
To copy is to transfer information to another location. The information is then being held in two places. Copy is a command in many **wordprocessing** programs. Text or a picture is copied and then moved to another part of the same page or file.
She copied the pages onto a floppy disk.

copy protection *noun*
Copy protection is a code put into some programs to prevent people using it without permission. A user cannot copy the program because the code stops the computer from carrying out the copy command.
Copy protection is often used in video games software.

copyright *noun*
Copyright is a law that protects the work of an author or artist. Copyright information cannot be used without asking permission. Software programs have a copyright. It is illegal to copy them without permission.
Working without a copyright is known as working copyright free.

corrupted data *noun*
Corrupted data is data that has errors in it. A problem in the hardware or software causes data to be lost or to be stored incorrectly. Corrupted data sometimes cannot be used.
Corrupted data looks like a jumble of symbols and letters.

CP/M *noun*
CP/M stands for Control Program/Monitor. This used to be the **operating system** in many **microcomputers**. CP/M was very popular, but newer operating systems were developed and have now taken its place.
Today, CP/M is seldom used.

CPS ► characters per second

CPU ► central processing unit

crash *noun*
A crash is when the computer stops working because of a fault in the hardware or software. Sometimes turning the computer off and **booting** it again will solve the problem. A crash may mean that a part of the computer must be repaired. A **head crash** means a problem with the **read-write heads**.
She lost hours of work because she had not saved her file before the computer crashed.
crash *verb*

cross talk *noun*
Cross talk is a term used in **telecommunications**. Cross talk is caused by **interference** on a telephone line. Interference on a telephone line can cause data loss.
Babble is another word for cross talk.

CRT ► **cathode ray tube**

cryogenic store *noun*
A cryogenic store is a type of **memory** being developed for **supercomputers**. It stores information at very low temperatures.
Scientists are still experimenting with cryogenic store.

current *noun*
Current is the rate of flow of electricity through a **circuit**. Some materials will allow an electric current to flow. These are **conductors**.
Electric current will flow through a conductor.

cursor *noun*
The cursor is a special character on the **visual display unit**. It shows where the user is working on the screen. The cursor can be moved using a **mouse**, or the arrow keys on a **keyboard**. It may be shaped like a block, a line, a finger, a cross or an arrow. Some software programs let the user design their own cursor.
A cursor shaped like a block can be set to blink off and on.

cut and paste *noun*
Cut and paste is a name given to moving text and images on a **visual display unit**. It is the electronic form of scissors and paste. Text or images are removed, or cut, from a page. They are then moved and pasted in a new location. Cut and paste can also be used to copy something.
He used cut and paste to move a paragraph from page one to page six.

cut-sheet feeder *noun*
A cut-sheet feeder is a device which takes one sheet of paper from a pile and feeds it into the printer. Many cut-sheet feeders will also handle envelopes. Many types of printer use a cut-sheet feeder.
The cut-sheet feeder was loaded with letterhead.

cybernetics *noun*
Cybernetics is the study of the way in which people control things. It also describes the way in which computers and other machines can be used to control something.
Cybernetic machines are designed to copy the actions a human would take to carry out a task. For example, a robot arm is designed to be able to move, pick things up and put them in the correct place.
Cybernetics is a very complex science.

cylinder *noun*
A cylinder is an area on a **disk pack**. It is the area on each disk that the **read-write heads** can read without moving.
The computer can read the contents of a cylinder with one spin of the disks.

disk pack

a
cylinder

39

daisy chain   *noun*
A daisy chain is a group of **peripheral** devices all connected through one **port** or **interface**. A **cable** is run to the first device. Another cable leads from the first device to a second, and so on.
The daisy chain connected the computer to a printer, a modem and a tape streamer.

daisy wheel printer   *noun*
A daisy wheel printer is a kind of **printer**. The part that actually puts the characters on the paper is a round device called a daisy wheel. The daisy wheel spins to the chosen character. A small hammer strikes the character against a ribbon, printing it onto the paper.
Daisy wheel printers have been replaced by laser, dot matrix and ink-jet printers.

DAT ▶ digital audio tape

data   *noun*
Data is information. It can take a number of forms, such as text or pictures. A **digital computer** stores and uses data as numbers.
A computer must have accurate data to work with if it is to produce good results.

data bank   *noun*
A data bank is a collection of **data bases**. It is stored in a computer, and is often available to users **on-line**. Information can be **retrieved** from a data bank by many people at the same time.
The information stored in a data bank usually refers to one subject or topic.

data capture   *noun*
Data capture is the process of putting information into a computer system so it can be processed. Data may be captured by typing it in, by using a digitizing camera, **scanner**, **optical character recognition**, **bar code** reader, or any similar device. Data may also be captured when a transaction takes place over **networked** systems.
Some methods of data capture are faster than others.

magnetic ink

cheque sorting machine

data communication   *noun*
Data communication is the process of moving, or transferring, information between computers. This is done through cables. Data communication may take place between computers in a **network**, or between two computers over a **modem**.
Coaxial cable is often used for data communication.

data compression   *noun*
Data compression is a way of changing the form in which data is stored, so that it takes up less **memory**. Data compression may also be used to reduce the time taken to send information over a **network** or **modem**. The original form can be brought back, or recovered. Data compression is often used for storing graphics or **video**.
With data compression, a floppy disk can hold much more information.

data conversion ▶ conversion program

data dictionary *noun*
A data dictionary is a file that contains the details of all the data used and processed by an **application** or set of applications.
The data dictionary is a useful tool for the systems analyst and programmer.

data entry ► **input**

data glove *noun*
A data glove is an input **device** which is worn on the hand. It has **sensors** which pick up information and pass it to a computer. The information may include the direction and the speed of a movement.
A data glove is worn on your hand like an ordinary glove.

data interchange format (DIF) *noun*
Data interchange format (DIF) is a **standard** arrangement for files. It is used in some software programs. Files in data interchange format can be moved, or **imported**.
Two software programs that use data interchange format can trade files.

data processing *noun*
Data processing is working with information using a computer. The term is most often used to refer to business or organizational jobs.
Many big companies have a data processing department.

data protection *noun*
Data protection is protecting people from problems caused by misuse of computer data. Many countries have laws on data protection. These laws may require organizations to register with the government if they keep information about individuals. The laws allow the individuals to see this information, and correct it if is wrong.
Data protection is especially important for keeping financial records confidential.

data structure *noun*
Data structure is the way in which groups of data are organized in a computer. For example, data may be kept in simple lists, or in rectangular tables. Some data is kept in more complicated structures, such as **trees** and **arrays**.
An array is an example of a data structure.

database *noun*
A database is a collection of information on a subject. The information can be changed and retrieved easily. Most database programs allow the user to **search** and look at the information in a number of different ways. The information about a particular item is held on a **record**. Each record may include a number of **fields** which hold specific details. There are two main arrangements of databases, **hierarchical databases** and **relational databases**.
The librarian searched an on-line database for information on new computer books.

database management system (DBMS) *noun*
A database management system is the software used to manage a **database**. It is this software that allows the data in a database to be entered, modified and **retrieved** in answer to queries. A database management system also allows **back up** copies of data to be taken.
Retrieval speed is very important in a large database management system.

date stamp *verb*
To date stamp is automatically to store the current date with information. Computer **operating systems** will date stamp a file to show when it was last changed.
When she closed the file, 18 April 1993 was date stamped.

deadly embrace *verb*
A deadly embrace is an error that can happen when computer **operating systems** or **programs** are not correctly written. It happens when one command is waiting for another command, which is waiting for another. The chain of waiting becomes a closed **loop**. This means that nothing in the loop will ever start. If this happens, the computer system may **crash** or lock up.
A deadly embrace is caused by a bug in a program.

debug *verb*
To debug is to make a program run properly. Sometimes, programs are not written correctly. The programmer debugs the program by finding where the error, or **bug**, is located and correcting it.
She had to debug the program because the cursor never appeared on the visual display unit.

decoder *noun*
A decoder is a device that changes coded data into unencoded data. The unencoded data is what the system or user can understand. For example, a decoder is needed before a television can display **teletext**.
A decoder can be a piece of hardware or a software program.

dedicated *adjective*
Dedicated describes something that is used for only one purpose. A dedicated computer system might be used only to run a special machine in a factory.
The business had a dedicated fax line from the computer to the telephone system.

default *noun*
A default is the way a computer or program works if the user does not make any changes. The computer looks at its default settings when it is turned on. The user can over-ride these default settings if a different choice is required. For example, **justification** and **insert** have a default set to off or on. A wordprocessing program usually opens a blank page and puts the cursor at the top left-hand corner of the page.
Most software programs include a default for a certain printer.
default *verb*

delete *verb*
To delete is to remove information. Files can be deleted from **memory**. The delete command in wordprocessing gets rid of text. Text and files that have been deleted accidentally can sometimes be restored.
He decided to delete a file of old business letters.
deletion *noun*

demo disk *noun*
A demo disk is a disk used to demonstrate **software**. It usually shows part of a program, or only lets the program carry out some of the operations. A demo disk is used to sell the software it demonstrates. It should encourage the user to buy the full, or unrestricted, **version** of the software.
Many magazines include a free demo disk with every issue.

demo disk

demodulator *noun*

A demodulator is a device that changes data signals. An **analog signal** is changed into a **digital signal**. This digital signal can then be used, or processed, by a computer.
A modem has both a modulator and a demodulator.

descending order *noun*

Descending order is an arrangement of a list. Numbers arranged in descending order start with the largest one and continue to the smallest. Words are put into descending order by starting with the end of the alphabet and continuing to the beginning.
The manager printed out a list of staff salaries in descending order.

desktop *noun*

A desktop is a display on a computer screen. It is used by some operating systems. The desktop display may show **icons**, **menus** to select from, **windows** to work in, and text within the windows. The icons show what programs and files can be opened immediately.
Her computer used a desktop to display the choices available.

device *noun*

A device is a piece of equipment. **Printers**, **keyboards** and **modems** are devices. In computer systems, devices are usually connected together by cables and wires.
A mouse is a device used to move the cursor.

device driver *noun*

A device driver is a program that tells a computer how to run a **device**. A mouse and a printer, for example, might need special software to communicate with the computer. The device driver gives the computer information such as the make and model of the device, what **baud rate** it runs on, and which **port** it is connected to.
She was able to use the mouse after the a driver was installed on the hard disk.

diagnostic test *noun*

A diagnostic test is a test used to check a system. If there is a problem with a piece of equipment, special **software** may be used to try to find information about the problem. The diagnostic test is designed to check each part of the equipment.
Some diagnostic tests can be run by a user, others only by trained staff.

dialog box *noun*

A dialog box is a box that appears on a computer screen. It is a rectangular box, containing text that gives information about a program or the operating system. For example, a dialog box might tell the user how much memory is available. Sometimes, the dialog box asks the user to make a choice. When the choice is made, the computer carries out the command.
The dialog box asked if he wanted to save the changes to the file.

dictionary *noun*

A dictionary is a book, or a file on a computer that contains a list of words. It gives the meaning of each word. A dictionary is included in most **wordprocessing** and **desktop publishing** programs. Words can be checked for spelling and easily replaced with the correct spelling.
She used the dictionary to see if she had spelled 'telecommunications' correctly.

43

desktop publishing *noun*

Desktop publishing is preparing text and pictures for printing, and then printing them. A typical system includes a **microcomputer**, desktop publishing **software**, a **mouse**, a **scanner** and a **laser printer**. All this equipment fits on a desk.

The desktop publishing course taught the students how to produce the school newspaper.

Publishing methods have changed with the introduction of new technology. Now, a microcomputer can be used to do many of the jobs a variety of machines used to do.

manual typewriter
author types text

typesetting machine
typesetter re-keys text

galleys
text printed in one long strip

paste-up
galleys and pictures arranged to fit the page

camera ready copy
plates made for the printing press

printing press

microcomputer
author types text straight to disk

scanner
pictures can be scanned in, or imported from other software packages

the page on screen
text and pictures can be moved around and re-sized to fit

laser printer

44

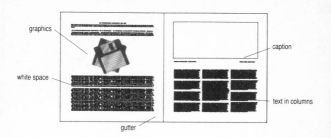

graphics

caption

white space

text in columns

gutter

A typeface is a set of letters, numbers and symbols with the same style.

ABCxyz
Americana

ABCxyz
Avant Garde

ABCxyz
Rockwell Bold

ABCxyz
Leawood Bold

Type is measured in point sizes. Six point type is difficult to read.

. 18 24 30 36 48 72

Leading is the amount of space between lines of text. The amount of leading can make a big difference to how easy a page is to read.

Without enough leading the text is very difficult to read. This is a sample of 14 point type with 8 points of leading.

Most text is set with one or two points of leading. This is a sample of 11 point type with one point of leading. It is described as 11 on 12, or 11/12.

Most text is set with one or two points of leading. This is a sample of 11 point type with two points of leading. It is described as 11 on 13, or 11/13.

Too much leading makes the text difficult to read. This is a sample of 10 point type with 20 points of leading.

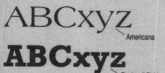

digit *noun*
A digit is a character used to write a number. Digits may be put together, or combined, to write larger numbers. In the decimal number system, the digits are 0, 1, 2, 3, 4, 5, 6, 7, 8 and 9. **Binary code** uses the digits 0 and 1. *The number 100 contains three digits.*
digital *adjective*

digital audio tape (DAT) *noun*
A digital audio tape (DAT) records data using a **digital signal**. A **gigabyte** of data can be put on a digital audio tape.
Digital audio tape is used for good quality sound recordings.

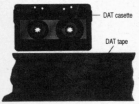

— DAT casette

DAT tape

digital camera *noun*
A digital camera is a camera that records pictures, or images, as **digital data**. Instead of using film which reacts to chemicals, the image is recorded on magnetic material. The process is called digital photography. The image may be displayed on a computer.
A picture taken with a digital camera can be looked at on a computer screen.

digital computer *noun*
A digital computer is a computer that can store and **process** information in the form of numbers, or **digits**. **Binary code** is used to change signals into digits, and digits into signals. A 0 means there is no **voltage**, or a switch is off. A 1 means there is voltage, or a switch is on. The term 'computer' is usually taken to mean a digital computer. The other form of computer is an **analog computer**.
Most computers today are digital computers.

digital data *noun*
Digital data is information recorded as a sequence of numbers, or **digits**. Digital computers store and **process** data in the form of numbers. Words, pictures and sounds are changed into digital form.
Digital data is used by most computers.

digital imaging *noun*
Digital imaging is the storage and use of pictures in digital form. Once the picture has been input using a **scanner** or **digitizer**, changes may be made. The image can be moved, or its size can be changed.
Digital imaging is used when pictures are taken of the inside of a person's body.

digital paper *noun*
Digital paper is a thin material that can be used for storing data. It is still at an experimental stage. Scientists think digital paper may become a cheap way to store large amounts of information. Digital paper can hold a **gigabyte** on a 51/4 inch disk.
Once information has been written on digital paper, it cannot be changed.

digital signal *noun*
A digital signal is a signal that is made up of on and off pulses of electricity. The **digit** 1 is used to stand for, or represent, on. The digit 0 is used to represent off. Most computers work using digital signals.
Digital signals can be changed to analog signals using a digital to analog converter.

digital to analog converter   *noun*
A digital to analog converter, or D/A
converter, is a device that changes a **digital
signal** into an **analog signal**.
A modem uses a digital to analog converter.

digital video interactive (DVI)   *noun*
Digital video interactive is a set way, or
format, for storing digital information on a
compact disk. Because it allows the user to
decide how to move through the information,
it is called interactive. Digital video
interactive handles information of various
kinds, including text, sound, video and other
pictures.
*Digital video interactive is only one format
used for compact disks.*

digitizer   *noun*
A digitizer is an electronic device in the form
of a pad or **tablet**. It is used with **graphics**
and **CAD** programs to **input** drawings from
paper into a computer. The user moves a
special pen or pointing device such as a
puck across the pad. Sensors in the pad
send digital information about the position of
the pointer to the computer.
*The architect drew the plans on the
computer using a digitizer.*

DIN plug   *noun*
A DIN plug is a type of **connector**. It is a
round plug with a number of pins in it. DIN
plugs must follow a **standard** which is used
internationally. DIN stands for Deutsche
Industrie Norm.
*A DIN plug is most often used to connect a
keyboard and a mouse.*

plug

connection
socket

dingbat   *noun*
A dingbat is a small picture or symbol. It can
be used to draw the attention of the reader.
Dingbats are used in desktop publishing.

dip switch   *noun*
A dip switch is a small switch used to
change the settings on a machine, or device.
Dip switches are often found in groups. For
example, one of the dip switches on a printer
may control the movement of the **platen**.
*A dip switch can usually be set in a number
of different positions.*

direct access memory   *noun*
Direct access memory is a type of **memory**
that stores information, or data, at an
address. Floppy disks and hard disks use
direct access memory.
RAM is direct access memory.

direct broadcasting by satellite (DBS)
noun
Direct broadcasting by satellite is the
sending of television signals by **satellite**.
The signal is sent to the satellite from the
broadcasting station. The satellite then
beams the signal to receiving dishes on
earth. **Cables** carry the signal from the
antenna to the television set. Direct
broadcasting by satellite can send one
television program to a very large area. This
area is called the **footprint**.
*Some radio stations also use direct
broadcasting by satellite.*

direct memory access (DMA) *noun*
Direct memory access is a way to move data between **storage devices**. It saves time by not going through the **central processing unit** first. The data moves directly between a disk or other device, and **RAM**.
Direct memory access is also known as random access.

directory *noun*
A directory is a list of files and other directories in a computer. It lists the name, the size, and often the date.
She looked at the directory to see how many bytes her wordprocessing files had used.

disable *verb*
To disable is to stop a device or prevent a software procedure from taking place.
A printer can be switched off in order to disable it.

disassembler *noun*
A disassembler is a program that changes **machine language** code into **assembly language**. It only works with **low level languages**.
Disassemblers are used to de-bug some kinds of program.

disk ► **floppy disk, hard disk**

disk drive *noun*
A disk drive is used to read information from, and write information to, a **hard disk**, **floppy disk** or **optical disk**. It spins, or rotates, the disk. The **read-write heads** of the disk drive are positioned over the part of the disk holding the information.
A floppy disk drive will not read an optical disk.

disk map *noun*
A disk map is a map used to keep track of the information on a disk. It is usually a **bit map** that tells the **operating system** which parts of a disk have been used.
The disk map recorded six full sectors.

disk mirroring *noun*
Disk mirroring is a method of sending data to two storage devices at the same time. This is done in case the computer **crashes** or one storage device does not work properly.
A software program is needed to carry out disk mirroring.

disk operating system ► **DOS**

disk pack *noun*
A disk pack is a group of **hard disks**. Each disk has a **read-write head**, but the group is treated as a single unit. A hard disk in a microcomputer is often a disk pack. Removable disk packs are often used with mainframe computers.
A removable disk pack is sealed inside a protective case.

mainframe disk pack

display *noun*
The display is the material that appears on the monitor, or **visual display unit**. This may be words or pictures. A display may be in colour or black and white.
The display showed part of a page of text.

display mode *noun*
The display mode is a setting that controls the type of information shown on a **visual display unit**. There are two display modes. The text display mode is used to show, or display characters. The graphics display mode is used to **display** pictures. The display mode also controls the detail, or **resolution**, of the screen.
The graphics display mode displays text as if it were a picture.

ocument *noun*
, document is a page, or collection of
ages, of information. A document may be
rinted on paper, or held in the computer's
memory. It can also be displayed on the
omputer screen.
*The wordprocessing directory listed 12
ocuments ready for printing.*

locument delivery *noun*
Document delivery is a service offered by
ome on-line databases. The user can order
a printed copy of a document in the
latabase.
*She used document delivery to get a copy of
the magazine article.*

locument image processing *noun*
Document image processing is a method
used to **input** information into a computer.
Documents are input using a **scanner** or a
digitizer. The document is held as a picture,
or image, rather than as characters in
computer code. In this way, details can be
stored as they appear on paper. For
example, a person's signature is stored as
they have written it.
*Many banks use document image
processing to keep a record of cheques.*

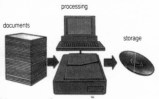

documents · processing · storage

documentation *noun*
Documentation is information that explains
hardware or software. It is usually in the
form of a book, or manual. Documentation is
important if a user wants to use a program
or device correctly.
*The documentation for the wordprocessing
program was a book and a chart.*

dongle *noun*
A dongle is a small piece of hardware used
to keep some programs from being copied.
The dongle is plugged into the computer.
Only then can the program be used. A copy
of the software cannot run without the same
dongle.
*Without the dongle, the database program
will not load.*

DOS *noun*
DOS is an **acronym** for Disk Operating
System. It is **system software** which is
loaded into the computer every time the
computer is turned on.
*DOS controls the movement of data
between disks.*

dot matrix *noun*
Dot matrix is a way of forming a character or
image from dots. It is used by some
displays and **dot matrix printers**. There
are usually 7, 9 or 18 dots for each in the
grid, or matrix.
*A dot matrix is made up of regularly spaced
dots.*

dot matrix printer *noun*
A dot matrix printer is a kind of **printer** that
uses dots to form characters on the paper.
Tiny pins press the ribbon onto the paper.
The pattern, or matrix, of the pins produces
the character on the page. Some dot matrix
printers can print simple graphics.
*Many dot matrix printers are very fast,
printing up to 500 characters per second.*

dots per inch (DPI) *noun*
Dots per inch is a measurement used to
describe **printers**. The dots per inch value is
the number of dots that the printer can print
in an inch. The more dots per inch the better
the quality, or **resolution**, of the printed
page.
*The print quality of a fax machine is also
measured in dots per inch.*

double density disk *noun*
A double density disk is a **floppy disk** that
can store twice as much as an ordinary
floppy disk.
*The abbreviation DD is often used to label
double density disks.*

double sided disk *noun*
A double sided disk is a **floppy disk** that
can hold data on both surfaces.
*The abbreviation DS is often used to label
double sided disks.*

down time *noun*
Down time is time during which a computer
cannot be used.
*Down time of computers in a business can
mean a loss of money.*

download *verb*
To download is to transfer information from a
computer to another device. A program or
data may be downloaded from a computer
to another computer, or to a printer.
*He used a modem to download the program
from the bulletin board.*

draft quality *noun*
Draft quality is a setting, or mode, on some
types of printer. It is the lowest **resolution** at
which a printer can print. Draft quality is the
quickest mode. It is often used for the first
printout, or draft, of a document.
*Draft quality is usually used when checking
a printout to see if any corrections are
necessary.*

DTP ► **desktop publishing**

dumb terminal ► **terminal**

dump *verb*
To dump is to send data to a storage device
for safe-keeping. All the files in the
computer's **memory**, or a specific part of the
computer's memory, are copied.
*She decided to dump the entire directory
onto the back up disk.*
dump *noun*

duplex *adjective*
Duplex describes a **transmission** that
allows a signal to be sent in two directions.
Full duplex systems allow signals to be sent
freely in both directions at the same time.
Half duplex allows signals to move in both
directions, but only one direction at a time.
A duplex signal can travel in both directions.

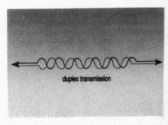

duplex transmission

DVI ► **digital video interactive**

50

E

earth station *noun*

An earth station is a large, dish-shaped **antenna** that sends and receives signals by way of a satellite. It is an important link in **telecommunications** networks.

The earth station picked up signals from the satellite 24 hours a day.

EBCDIC *noun*

EBCDIC is a code used to stand for, or represent, characters. EBCDIC is the **acronym** for Extended Binary Coded Decimal Interchange Code.

EBCDIC is pronounced eeb-see-dick.

echo *noun*

An echo is a subject area on a **bulletin board**. Each echo contains information about a certain topic.

The games echo sometimes has hints about how to win video games.

edge connector *noun*

An edge connector is part of some **circuit boards**. It connects the board to the **motherboard**. Thin strips of metal called **conductors** run to the edge connector. The conductors pass signals to and from the computer by way of the edge connector.

The edge connector should be firmly slotted into position.

edit *verb*

To edit is to change something, usually for the better. Both words and pictures can be edited.

The artist loaded the graphics program in order to edit the picture.

editor *noun*

An editor is a program that is used to change information held in files. A text editor is like a **wordprocessor**, but is only concerned with the characters and not with they way they look. Editors are often used to type or change programs or numerical data. There are also editors for changing pictorial, or graphical, data. A **pixel** editor can be used to change data pixel by pixel.

She used a text editor to change the batch file of the computer.

EGA ► **enhanced graphics adaptor**

Eighty-column display *noun*

An eighty-column display is a **visual display unit** on which a maximum of 80 characters can be shown on one line. Many older dumb terminals had this maximum limit.

The eighty-column display could not show the entire spreadsheet.

eject *verb*

To eject is to remove something. A microcomputer will eject a 5¼-inch **floppy disk** when the drive door is opened. A 3½-inch disk is ejected by pressing a button on the outside of the drive.

The activity light must be out before it is safe to eject a floppy disk.

electronic funds transfer *noun*

Electronic funds transfer is a method of sending money between banks and customers. **Telecommunications** are used to send details about the transaction. The banks put money in an account, or take it out, as instructed.

In electronic funds transfer, no one need actually handle paper or paper money.

51

electronic mail *noun*
Electronic mail is a way of sending messages between people using a computer or computers on a network. The message or document can be looked at on a computer screen, and printed out.
Electronic mail is often shortened to email.

electronic messaging *noun*
Electronic messaging is the term used to describe all forms of communication using computers. For example, **electronic mail**, **videotext** and **voice messaging** are all types of electronic messaging.
Electronic messaging is used by many businesses.

electronics *noun*
Electronics is the study of the behaviour of electrons in electronic circuits. It is based upon the way electrons move between and through different materials.
The hardware for telecommunications devices and computers depends on the study of electronics.

email ► **electronic mail**

embedded computer *noun*
An embedded computer is a computer which is part of a machine designed for one particular purpose. The embedded computer controls the machine.
Many cameras and video recorders have an embedded computer.

emulate *verb*
To emulate means to act like something else. Some types of **printer** can emulate other printers. The printer follows the same instructions and prints just as the other printer would.
A new computer can emulate an older one.

emulator *noun*
An emulator is a **program** that makes one computer behave as if it were another type of computer.
An emulator can allow new computers to run older software without re-programming.

enable *verb*
To enable is to set up **hardware** or a **program** so that it can work.
Enable is the opposite of disable.

encrypt *verb*
To encrypt is to put data into a code. This is done so that the data cannot be read or understood by an unauthorized person. An authorized person is given a key, such as a special code word, or number. The key **enables** a program to put the information back into its original **form**.
The bank's rule is to encrypt all private and confidential information.
encryption *noun*

end key *noun*
The end key is a key found on many computer **keyboards**. Pressing it usually places the **cursor** at the end of a line, a page or a file. It can be programmed for other purposes.
It is faster to press the end key than to move across the page using the right arrow key.

end of text character *noun*
The end of text character is a special character used to mark the end of the text in a **transmission**. It tells the receiving device that a message is complete.
The end of text character appears after the last word in a message.

end user   *noun*
The end user is the person who uses a
program or computer. This is the person at
the end of a long chain of people who design
and make computer products. The end user
is usually the person who buys the product.
*The real test of a new video game is how
much enjoyment it gives the end user.*

enhance   *verb*
To enhance is to make something better, or
make it stand out. Computer systems can be
enhanced by adding on **hardware**. Text can
be enhanced by printing it bold or
underlined. A **multimedia** presentation can
be enhanced by adding a soundtrack.
*He enhanced his system by replacing the
black and white monitor with a colour
monitor.*

enhanced graphics adaptor (EGA)
noun
An enhanced graphics adaptor is an
electronic circuit which allows text and
graphics in up to 16 colours to be displayed
on the screen at the same time. It is made
following a **standard**, so it can be used with
many visual display units.
*The CAD program needed a computer with
an enhanced graphics adaptor.*

enter   *verb*
To enter is to put information into a
computer, usually through the **keyboard**.
*Some computer systems require the user to
enter a password before they can use the
system.*

enter key   *noun*
The enter key is a key on a computer
keyboard. It is used to indicate that a
command is complete and ready to be
carried out. In most **wordprocessing**
programs, the enter key carries out a **hard
return**. This allows the typist to begin a new
line or paragraph.
*Pressing the enter key moves the cursor to
the beginning of a new line.*

envelope   *noun*
1. An envelope is the information or codes
used so that a message can be **transmitted**
correctly. The envelope does not include the
message itself.
*Messages sent over telecommunications
systems use an envelope.*
2. An envelope holds information about a
sound or musical note. The envelope
describes how a particular sound changes.
The computer can control the sound using
the envelope.
*In the music program, each sound is held in
its own envelope.*

environment   *noun*
The environment in information technology
is the combination of hardware and software
being used in a **computer system**. Software
written for one computer **operating system**
will not run on another if the environment is
different.
*Different versions of a software program are
often available for a number of
environments.*

EPROM   *noun*
EPROM is the **acronym** for Erasable
Programmable Read Only Memory. It is
memory used to store information that stays
the same, or that rarely needs to be
changed. To change the information on an
EPROM, it must be taken from the computer
and put into a special device. The entire
contents of the EPROM are **deleted**, and it
is ready to be programmed again.
*An EPROM is erased by exposing the chip
to ultraviolet light.*

ergonomic   *adjective*
Ergonomic describes equipment that has
been designed to be comfortable and safe to
use. An ergonomic chair supports the user's
back and can be adjusted up and down.
*The workstation was comfortable because of
its ergonomic design.*
ergonomics   *noun*

error   *noun*
An error is a mistake. An error, or **bug**, in a
software program or in computer hardware
can cause the computer to **crash**. An error
in typing may cause a wrong result it is not
noticed and changed.
*Trying to copy a file to a disk drive that is
empty causes an error.*

error message   *noun*
An error message is a message given when
something is not done correctly, or the
computer is unable to carry out a **command**.
It is often displayed in an **alert box**.
*He tried to print a file but the error message
'Printer not connected' came up on the
visual display unit.*

escape   *verb*
To escape is to stop a program from running
or to return to the previous display on the
visual display unit. It is a **command** used to
cancel the last choice, or close a menu.
*To stop data being sent to the printer the
user must escape from the command.*

escape key   *noun*
The escape key is a key on a computer
keyboard. It is used to carry out an escape
command. The escape key often has the
abbreviation 'Esc' written on it. It is usually
close to the **function keys** at the top of the
keyboard.
*She pressed the escape key to cancel her
last command.*

execute   *verb*
To execute is to carry out a program or
instructions. A program is executed when it
begins to run. It continues executing until the
user exits the program.
*A command is executed by pressing the
enter key or clicking a mouse button.*

exit   *verb*
1. To exit is to close, or leave, a software
program.
*The students were taught to exit from the
software program before switching off the
computer.*
2. To EXIT in **programming language** is to
leave a **subroutine**. The programmer may
then continue with the main part of the
program.
*It is necessary to exit a subroutine before a
new subroutine is run.*

expanded memory   *noun*
Expanded memory is extra **RAM** that can be
added to some microcomputers. It is used to
store data. The expanded memory may be
added as a **SIMM**.
*Expanded memory gives the computer more
than the usual 640K of RAM.*

expansion board   *noun*
An expansion board is a **circuit board** that
is added to the **motherboard** in a computer.
It fits into an **expansion slot**. The expansion
board may be a modem, provide additional
memory, or give the computer other added
capabilities.
*An expansion board is also called an
expansion card.*

expansion card ► expansion board

expansion slot *noun*
An expansion slot is a slot where an **expansion board** may be fitted. The slot is connected to the **bus** on a **motherboard**.
In order to fit an expansion board, there must be an empty expansion slot.

expert system *noun*
An expert system is a **computer system** that holds all the available information about a subject, together with a program that allows the information to be used. The program asks the user questions, and can suggest solutions to problems.
An expert system can be used in medicine to help find out what is wrong with a patient.

export *verb*
To export is to send data from one software program to another software program, or from one computer to another computer. Text and pictures, or graphics, can be exported.
She exported a picture of a dinosaur from a graphics program so she could use it in her desktop publishing program.

expression *noun*
1. An expression is a combination of **operations** in a **programming** language. Two or more operations are grouped together in an expression.
The programmer had to correct the last expression in the program.
2. An expression is a mathematical equation that represents a value in a computer program. For example, C=A+B is an expression.
Expressions are used in most programs.

extended memory *noun*
Extended memory is extra **RAM** that can be added to some microcomputers. It is used by **systems software**.
Extended memory gives the computer more than one megabyte of RAM.

external back up *noun*
An external back up is a copy of a file or files kept on a **storage device** outside a computer. If anything goes wrong with the computer, the data is still safe and available. An external back up helps to protect data from **viruses** or other problems on a hard disk.
The data processing department uses a tape drive to store their external back up.

tape back up

extra density disk *noun*
An extra density disk is a **floppy disk** that can be formatted to hold up to four **megabytes**.
Extra density disks are available in $3\frac{1}{2}$ inch and $5\frac{1}{4}$ inch sizes.

F

facsimile transmission ► **fax**

fanfold stationery ► **continuous stationery**

fatal error *noun*
A fatal error is a mistake, or **error**, that causes a computer to **crash**. The problem can be in the hardware or in the software. The error must be corrected for the computer to operate properly again. A 'fatal error' message will usually appear on the screen.
A missing line of programming caused a fatal error.

fax ► page 57

fault *noun*
A fault is something that stops a device from working properly. It may also be a **bug** in a program. Finding out what is causing a fault is called **troubleshooting**.
The engineer traced the fault to a loose connection.

female *adjective*
Female describes a socket that has holes in it. It is a type of **connector**.
Connectors can be described as either male or female.

female socket

fibre optics *plural noun*
Fibre optics is the use of special cables made of a material similar to glass. Data is sent as pulses of light through the cables. Fibre optic cables carry many more signals than ordinary cables of the same size.
In fibre optics, electric pulses are changed into pulses of light.

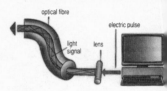

optical fibre

electric pulse

light signal

lens

field *noun*
A field is part of a **record** in a **database**. It is a separate area used to hold information. Each field has a name. For example, a database of addresses would include a 'post code' field. *Information in a database can be arranged, or sorted, by field.*

field delimiter *noun*
A field delimiter is a special character used to show where a **field** ends. It sets a limit to the length of a field.
A comma is often used as a field delimiter.

fifth generation computer *noun*
Fifth generation computer is a name given to computers now being designed and developed. They will work using **expert systems** and **artificial intelligence**.
Many scientists are working on the development of fifth generation computers.

file *noun*
A file is a unit of information. A computer file may hold a document such as a letter, a group of database **records** or a program. The contents of a file may be held in many different **clusters** on a hard or floppy disk.
Every file on a computer has a name.

fax *noun*

1. A fax, or facsimile, is a **telecommunications** device which transmits documents or pictures as electronic signals. Another fax receives the signals and either prints them out or displays them on a computer. There are desktop fax machines, portable faxes for computers and internal faxes which can be fitted into a computer.
The fax is one of the machines used the most in an office.

2. A fax, or facsimile, is a document or picture sent as an electronic signal over the telephone system. The document or picture can be on a piece of paper or on a computer.
A fax is an electronic copy of a document.

telephone fax

portable fax

connects to telephone cable

connects to computer port

internal fax

connects to motherboard

fitted inside computer

Portable and internal faxes send and receive signals straight from or to a computer.

57

file extension   *noun*
A file extension is an addition to a **file name**.
It is usually three characters that follow a full
stop. The file extension is used to describe
the **format** of the data in the file. For
example, the extension .txt is often used for
a text file.
*The file extension .bat in zip.bat means that
zip is a batch file.*

file management   *noun*
File management is the organization of files
on a **storage device**. File management
includes naming files, **backing up** files and
organizing files in **directories**.
*Proper file management is very important in
large businesses with millions of files.*

file name   *noun*
A file name is a name given to a **file** so that
it can be found, or **retrieved**. It usually gives
some information about what is in the file.
Each file must have a different name.
*She gave the file name 'car' to her letter
about car insurance.*

file protection   *noun*
File protection is a way of stopping a **file**
from being accidentally deleted from a
storage device. Floppy disks have a hole or
notch in their case. If the hole is covered, the
computer will not write data to the disk. A
reel of computer tape has a file protect ring.
If this plastic ring is removed, the computer
will not write data to the tape.
*File protection is especially important for
new program disks.*

file server   *noun*
A file server is a computer that holds
information, or files, for other computers.
In a **network**, the file server has a large
capacity hard disk. The other computers in
the network **access** the file server to store
and retrieve files.
*The file server in a network must be
powerful enough to handle files from all the
other computers.*

file transfer   *noun*
A file transfer is the movement of a **file** from
one computer to another. The file is sent
using a modem, or to another computer in a
network. Special software must be used
when the **computer systems** are not
compatible.
*File transfer takes place between computers
in a network.*
file transfer   *verb*

firmware   *noun*
Firmware is data and programs that are built
into a computer. It is held in **ROM** on an
integrated circuit and cannot be changed
by the user. Firmware usually holds parts of
the **operating system** and instructions for
input and **output devices**.
Firmware is a type of software.

fixed disk ► **hard disk**

fixed point arithmetic   *noun*
Fixed point arithmetic is one way a computer
uses numbers for arithmetic calculations.
The computer fixes the decimal point in the
same position for every number. Only a
certain number of **digits** may be used.
*Fixed point arithmetic is fast, but cannot
handle very large numbers.*

flag   *noun*
A flag is a marker or signal that tells the
computer that a certain thing has, or has not,
happened. For example, a flag tells the
computer when all the data in a file has been
copied.
*A flag tells the computer when a printer is
ready to receive data.*

flatbed plotter   *noun*
A flatbed plotter is a type of **plotter** that
draws on paper held on a flat board. Flatbed
plotters are used to output technical
drawings from **CAD** programs. Some of
them are quite small, but others can plot a
large map on a single sheet of paper.
Most flatbed plotters are pen plotters.

flicker *noun*

Flicker is an uneven glow of light on a **visual display unit**. It usually happens when the screen is not being **refreshed** quickly enough, or if it is not being refreshed at a steady rate.

Too much flicker on a display can cause eyestrain.

flicker *verb*

flip-flop *verb*

A flip-flop is a **circuit** that can be in one of two states.

An electric pulse will change a flip-flop to its opposite state.

floating point arithmetic *noun*

Floating point arithmetic is one way a computer uses numbers for arithmetic calculations. The computer keeps track of the point as it moves, or floats, from one position to another as the numbers get larger or smaller.

Floating point arithmetic is used when calculations must be very accurate.

floppy disk ► page 60

floptical disk *noun*

A floptical disk is a **floppy disk** used in a special **disk drive** that uses light, or optics, to read and write data. A floptical disk drive is far more accurate than the **read-write heads** in an ordinary disk drive. This lets a floptical disk hold far more data than an ordinary floppy disk of the same size.

A lens focuses light on a floptical disk to read data from it.

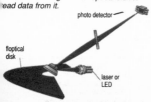

floptical disk

photo detector

laser or LED

flowchart *noun*

A flowchart is a diagram or map showing the steps taken to reach a certain result. Flowcharts can show how information moves from one part of a computer system to another. They can also show how one **instruction** in a **program** leads to another. Flowcharts contain boxes of different shapes connected by lines.

Special symbols stand for certain things on a computer flowchart.

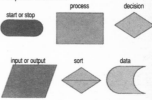

start or stop   process   decision

input or output   sort   data

folder *noun*

A folder is a collection of **files**. Some software uses a **subdirectory** instead of a folder.

His letters to friends were kept in a folder named 'My Favourite People'.

font *noun*

A font is a set of characters that have the same features. Each font is made up of a complete **character set** in a certain **typeface** and **typestyle**. For example, 12 point Helvetica Bold is a font. All of the characters in a font are designed to look similar. Computer fonts are often **bit map** fonts. They are used in **desktop publishing** programs.

New fonts can be bought and added to a desktop publishing package.

footer *noun*

A footer is information that is printed at the bottom, or foot, of a page.

She typed a command that put the date as a footer on each page in the document.

floppy disk *noun*

A floppy disk is a circular piece of thin,
flexible plastic inside a protective case. The
disk is coated with a film containing iron
particles. These particles are magnetized
when **data** is written to the disk. Particles
pointing, or aligned, one way record a zero.
Those aligned the other way record a one.
Single sided disks hold data on one side.
Double sided disks hold data on both sides.
A floppy disk is a type of magnetic memory.

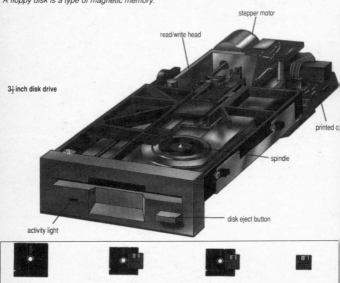

stepper motor

read/write head

$3\frac{1}{4}$ inch disk drive

printed c

spindle

disk eject button

activity light

8 inch disks
single sided, single density (SS/SD) 400Kb
single sided, double density (SS/DD) 800Kb
double sided, double density (DS/DD) 1500Kb

double sided, double density (DS/DD)
$5\frac{1}{4}$-inch disks 500Kb
$3\frac{1}{2}$-inch disks 1Mb

high density (HD)
$5\frac{1}{4}$-inch disks 1.6Mb
$3\frac{1}{2}$-inch disks 2Mb

extra density (ED)
$3\frac{1}{2}$-inch disks 4Mb

The capacity of a floppy disk depends on the drive used to format it. A formatted disk will hold less because formatting uses up some of the memory.

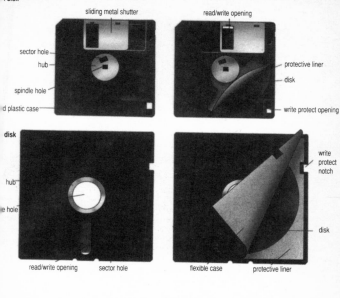

h disk

sliding metal shutter

read/write opening

sector hole

hub

spindle hole

d plastic case

protective liner

disk

write protect opening

disk

hub

e hole

read/write opening   sector hole

write protect notch

disk

flexible case   protective liner

ted disk

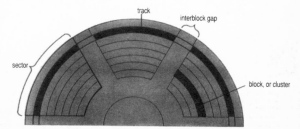

track   interblock gap

sector

block, or cluster

footprint   noun

1. A footprint is the area that a transmission from a satellite can reach.
The footprint covers most of the eastern United States of America.

2. A footprint is the amount of space a computer takes up on a desk or workspace.
His computer had a small footprint and fitted easily onto his desk.

form   noun

A form is a piece of paper that has questions printed on it. Empty spaces are left for answers. A database can be set up to print the answers in the space provided.
The database displays a copy of the form on screen, so it is easy for the user to input answers.

form feed   noun

A form feed is a **command** that moves the piece of paper in a printer all the way through so that the paper can be removed. When the printer is loaded with **continuous paper**, a form feed moves the paper to the top of the next page.
A form feed command can be given by pressing a button on the printer.

form letter   noun

A form letter is a letter in which different pieces of information can be placed by a **wordprocessing** or **database** program. The form letter contains all the text that will remain the same. Special codes are placed in the form letter. These codes tell the computer to take information from an address file or database file and place it in the form letter.
Form letters are used for mailshots.

format   noun

The format is the way information is organized in order to be stored, displayed or printed. A printer is given instructions by a computer about where to print information on a page. A floppy disk used with one make of computer may not store data in the same way, or format, as a floppy disk used with another computer. The format must be the same for the disk to be **compatible**.
The format of a floppy disk determines which computers it can be used in.

format   verb

1. To format is to prepare a disk so that it can store information. Formatting a disk puts **tracks** and **sectors** on it which will hold data. A special **utility program** is run to format a disk.
She needed to format another disk so she could back up her files.
2. To format is to prepare a page to look a certain way. In a **wordprocessing** file, formatting may include setting the margins, changing the line spacing and turning the **justification** on or off.
He decided to format the page using double spacing.

formula   (plural **formulae**)   noun

A formula is a rule in mathematics using symbols. It can be used to solve a calculation. For example, $X = 2 \times Y$ is a formula.
The programmer used a formula in the first instruction of the program.

FORTRAN *noun*

FORTRAN is the **acronym** for FORmula TRANslator. It is a **programming language** used mainly for science and mathematics programs.

FORTRAN is a high level language.

Fourth generation language (4GL) *noun*

Fourth generation languages are powerful **programming languages**. They need fewer **statements** than earlier programming languages to carry out the same instructions.

Fourth generation languages are easier and faster to use than earlier languages.

fragmentation *noun*

Fragmentation describes what happens when data from a file is split up over too many places on a storage disk. The contents of a file are stored in different **clusters** on a disk. When a file is saved over and over again, different parts of the file are saved in many different places. This results in fragmentation.

There are special programs that will get rid of fragmentation.

frame *noun*

1. A frame is one screen of **teletext** or **videotex**.
She used the keypad to change the frame of teletext.

2. A frame is one picture, or image, from a video or motion picture film.
A sequence of frames makes up a moving picture.

one frame

freeze frame video *noun*

Freeze frame video is **video** that only records one picture, or **frame**, every few seconds or minutes. The picture only changes after a set period of time, instead of continuously like a **full motion video**.

Freeze frame video can be sent over telephone lines.

frequency *noun*

Frequency is how often something happens. The frequency of a signal is measured in cycles per second, or **hertz**.

The frequency of a signal is shown by how close together waves are in a diagram.

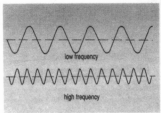

low frequency

high frequency

frequency modulation ► **modulation**

full duplex ► **duplex**

full motion video *noun*

Full motion video is **video** that records or plays a continuously changing picture. Many **multimedia** systems display full motion video.

Computers with a video card and special software can edit full motion video.

full text retrieval *noun*

Full text retrieval is a method of searching a **database**. The user types in the text to **search** for and the computer program locates it. Any word or group of words in the file can be used to search the text.

Full text retrieval is the easiest way for a beginner to search a database.

function *noun*
A function is a job, or task, for the computer to carry out. In **programming**, a function is a **routine** or a **subroutine**.
In one programming language, the function instruction 'SQR 9' will find the square root of nine.

function key *noun*
A function key is one of a group of keys on a computer **keyboard**. Each one is labelled with the letter F and a number. Pressing a function key will carry out different jobs, or **functions**, depending on the software program being used. Function keys can also be programmed by the user. They are usually along the top, or down one side, of the keyboard.
Most computer keyboards have 12 function keys numbered from F1 to F12.

garbage *noun*
Garbage is information, or data, which is no longer needed by a user. Garbage should be deleted whenever regular **housekeeping** is carried out.
All the garbage on his hard disk made it difficult for him to find the file he wanted.

garbage in garbage out (GIGO) *noun*
Garbage in garbage out is a popular expression used as a warning. It means that if poor work is put into a computer, poor work will come out of it.
Garbage in garbage out is sometimes abbreviated to GIGO.

gas plasma display *noun*
A gas plasma display is a type of screen display that sends an electric current through a special gas to form characters on the screen.
Many portable computers have a gas plasma display.

gate *noun*
A gate is a switch that either lets an electronic pulse pass through, or blocks it. The gate does this according to the instructions in a **truth table**.
There are different types of gate, including the AND gate, OR gate and NOT gate.

gateway *noun*
A gateway is a device that lets computers in one **network** work with computers in a different network.
A gateway has its own memory and processor.

Gbyte ► **gigabyte**

gender changer *noun*
A gender changer is a type of **adaptor** that can be used to connect **cables**. It changes a **female** socket into a **male** plug, or a male plug into a female socket.
A gender changer can be used to make a plug and socket compatible.

female   male

generation *noun*
A generation is all the hardware made using the same basic technology. For example, the first generation of computers used vacuum tubes. Second generation computers used transistors. Third generation computers used the first integrated circuits. Fourth generation computers use integrated circuits made using **very large scale integration**.
Scientists are now working on fifth generation computers.

giga- *prefix*
Giga- is a prefix used at the beginning of a word to mean one thousand million.
Gigahertz means one thousand million hertz.

gigabyte (Gbyte) *noun*
A gigabyte is a unit of measurement of computer **memory**. A gigabyte is made up of one thousand million **bytes**. Computers use **binary code**, so a gigabyte is 2^{30} or 1,073,741,824 bytes.
Some hard disks hold over a gigabyte of data.

GIGO ► **garbage in garbage out**

glare *noun*
Glare is light reflected from a visual display unit. It may be from a window or an electric light. A special filter can be used to cut down glare.
Glare can cause headache or eyestrain.

glitch *noun*
A glitch is **interference** on a television screen. A horizontal line, or bar, moves from the bottom of the screen to the top.
A glitch was so annoying, he turned the television off.

global *adjective*
Global describes something that includes everything. In programming, a global **variable** has the same value throughout the whole program. A global **search** will search an entire file. A global **back up** will back up all the files on a hard disk.
She used a global search to find the word 'torch'.

grandfather-father-son *noun*
Grandfather-father-son is a way of making sure that **files** on **back up** disks or tapes are safe. A new disk or tape back up is made each time a file is **updated**. The 'son' is the newest copy. If something happens to the data in the 'son' file, the 'father' file can be used. If something happens to the 'father' file, the 'grandfather' file can be used.
When the file was corrupted, the grandfather-father-son copies restored the data.

graph *noun*
A graph is a diagram used to display information. The information is to do with numbers, or is **numerical**. Business **graphics** and many **spreadsheet** programs are used to produce graphs on a computer. There are many different types of graphs, including pie charts, bar graphs and line graphs. Computers can display three-dimensional graphs.
The graph showed the temperatures for each month in London, Tokyo and Chicago.

graphics *plural noun*

Graphics are pictures, drawings or diagrams. Graphics programs are used to produce these images on a computer. The images can be two-dimensional or three-dimensional. **Animation** is used to produce moving images.

A colour display is needed to see computer graphics at their best.

A drawing or paint package lets the user work with different colours, shapes and lines.

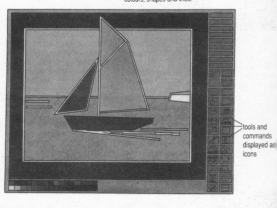

tools and commands displayed as icons

Computer animation is used in many computer games.
A moving picture is displayed on the screen.

Business graphics programs are often included in spreadsheet and database packages. They are used to display numerical information on charts or graphs.

CAD, or computer aided design, programs can be used to produce three-dimensional images. They can be simple geometric shapes or very complicated drawings.

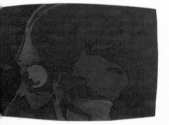

Various types of computer graphics are used in medicine. Scanners and sensors are used to input data. A computer program puts together an image from the data.

graph plotter ► **plotter**

graphical user interface (GUI) *noun*
A graphical user interface is one way computers are designed to make them easy to use, or **interface** with. It uses pictures, or icons, and menus.
WIMP is another term used for graphical user interface.

graphics ► page 66

graphics card *noun*
A graphics card is a special **circuit board** that can be fitted into an **expansion slot** in a computer. It gives the computer the **functions** it needs to run **graphics** programs.
A graphics card is needed to run CAD programs.

graphics mode *noun*
Graphics mode is a setting from a **visual display unit**. It is used to display pictures, but can also display text. The text is treated as a shape, or picture.
Graphics mode will display text, but text mode cannot display pictures.

graphics tablet *noun*
A graphics tablet is an **input device** that uses a pad, or tablet, and a special pen. The user draws on the tablet, and measurements of the lines are sent to the computer. Some graphics tablets also have boxes holding commands. The user can select a command with the **puck**.
A graphics tablet can be used to trace drawings, or to draw freehand.

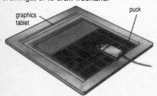

graphics tablet

puck

grey scale *noun*
The grey scale is a table of the amounts of black and white used to make different shades of grey. **Printers**, **scanners** and **visual display units** use the grey scale. The grey scale is especially useful for working with black and white photographs.
In a grey scale, different amounts of black and white are mixed to give different shades of grey.

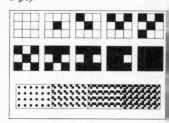

greyed *adjective*
Greyed describes a choice, or item, on a **menu** that cannot be used. The item looks light grey compared to the rest of the choices. **Clicking** on a greyed item gets no results.
The user must be in the right part of a program to use a greyed item.

GUI ► **graphical user interface**

gutter *noun*
The gutter is the area running down the side of a page that is going to be next to another page. It is left blank so that the text on the left-hand page is not too close to the text on the right-hand page.
The user must remember to allow for the gutter when designing pages with a desktop publishing program.

H

hacker *noun*
A hacker was originally a **programmer** who did not work for a particular company. Today, hacker is used to mean someone who gains **access** to computer programs or systems without permission.
Some hackers cause damage to valuable data or spread viruses.
hack *verb*

half duplex *noun*
Half duplex is a transmission system which allows data to travel in both directions, but one direction at a time.
The dumb terminal and the computer use half duplex to communicate.

hand-held *adjective*
Hand-held describes something small enough to hold in one hand. Examples of hand-held devices include computers, scanners, calculators, video games and television sets.
Microelectronics makes it possible to build many hand-held devices.

handshake *noun*
A handshake is a number of **signals** sent between two devices to make sure they are ready to exchange information. For example, a computer exchanges a handshake with a printer, fax or modem connected to it. If the handshake is not completed, the computer will not be able to communicate with the device.
A handshake makes sure that a peripheral, such as a printer, can receive data from a computer.

hard card *noun*
A hard card is a **hard disk** on a **circuit board**. A hard card is fitted into an **expansion slot** in a **microcomputer**. It is used to add more **memory**.
A hard card can be fitted to a computer that only has a floppy disk drive.

hard copy *noun*
Hard copy is information from a file printed on paper.
A hard copy of the price list was kept next to the cash register.

hard disk ► page 70

hard sector *noun*
A hard sector is an area of a hard or **floppy disk**. Hard sectors are recorded on the disk by the manufacturer when it is made.
The opposite of a hard sector is a soft sector.

hard space *noun*
A hard space is a space the user types in using the space bar on a computer **keyboard**. For example, a hard space is put between two words.
The computer will not get rid of a hard space unless the user deletes it.

hardware *noun*
Hardware is computer equipment. It includes all the **components** used to make the computer. It also includes the **cables**, **connectors** and computer **peripherals**. Most of a computer system is hardware, but programs are **software**.
Hardware is anything that can be picked up.

HD disk ► high density disk

head *noun*
A head is a device that **reads** or **writes** information from a **hard disk** or **floppy disk**. It moves in and out over the disk to find the data.
A head is also called a read-write head.

hard disk *noun*

A hard disk is a solid, round disk or a
number of these disks. When there is more
than one disk, each one is called a platter.
The disks are made of a magnetic material,
and are sealed inside a case. Hard disks are
memory devices used by most computers.
*There are between 1 and 12 platters in a
hard disk.*

Tiny hard disks are used in laptop and other small
computers. This one is about the size of a box of matches.

**microcomputer hard disk and
drive**

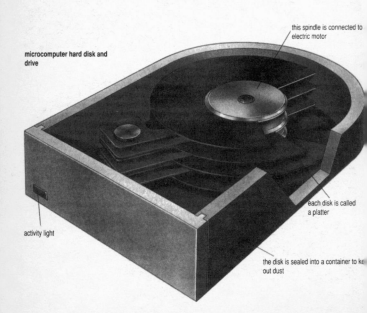

this spindle is connected to
electric motor

each disk is called
a platter

activity light

the disk is sealed into a container to ke
out dust

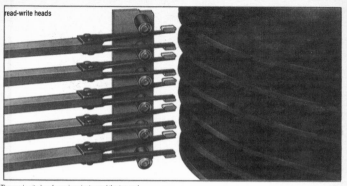

read-write heads

The read-write heads are in pairs to read the top and bottom surface of each platter.

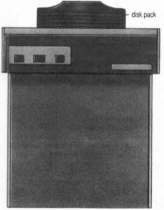

disk pack

mainframe disk drive

disk pack

A mainframe computer uses a disk pack on each disk drive. The disks are sealed into a container to protect them from dust, and to make them easy to change.

head crash *noun*

A head crash is a problem caused by a read-write **head** hitting the disk. The heads are positioned very close to the disk when they are reading or writing data. If they touch the disk, data can be lost or the disk can be damaged.

A dust particle, or even a fingerprint, can cause a head crash.

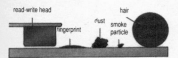

header *noun*

A header is information printed at the top of a page.

'Top Secret' was the header on each page of the report.

help *noun*

Help is information that is included as part of a software program. Most software has a help **menu** which is used to choose a subject. The help is displayed on the screen.

She looked at the help screen to see how to merge a document.

hertz (Hz) *noun*

Hertz is a unit of measurement. It measures **frequency** in cycles per second.

A computer's speed is usually measured in millions of hertz.

hexadecimal notation *noun*

Hexadecimal notation is a system of arithmetic based on 16. It uses the ten **digits** 0 to 9, and the letters A to F. Each hexadecimal digit stands for, or represents, four **bits**. A **byte** is represented by two hexadecimal digits. Hexadecimal notation is shorter than **binary code** which uses eight digits to represent a byte.

The decimal number 26 is written as 1A in hexadecimal notation.

hidden file *noun*

A hidden file is a **file** that is not listed in a directory, even though it is there. A hidden file usually contains program instructions that the user must not change.

A hidden file cannot be copied or erased from a disk.

hierarchical database *noun*

A hierarchical database is a database that is arranged in a **tree**. There is only one path to the items in the database. The path starts with a broad subject, and leads to more specific items.

Some graphics and CAD programs keep clip art in a hierarchical database.

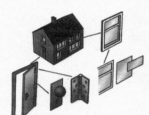

high density disk *noun*

A high density disk is a type of **floppy disk**. A $5\frac{1}{4}$ inch high density disk can be **formatted** to hold 1.2 **megabytes**. A $3\frac{1}{2}$ inch high density disk can be formatted to hold 1.4 megabytes.

A high density disk can hold more data than a double density disk.

high level language *noun*

A high level language is a **programming language** in which each instruction stands for several instructions in **machine code**. The high level language must go through an **interpreter** or **compiler** to put it into machine code. The computer can then carry out the instructions.

COBOL, FORTRAN and BASIC are high level languages.

high resolution *adjective*

High resolution describes **printers**, **visual display units** and **scanners** that work with a large number of **dots per inch**. The more dots, or **pixels**, per inch, the more accurately the device works.

The artist needed a high resolution visual display unit to work on a detailed drawing.

hit rate *noun*

The hit rate is a measurement of how successful a user is when carrying out a **search** in a **database**. It is the number of **records** or **character strings** found during a search.

An experienced user will have a higher hit rate than a beginner.

Hollerith card *noun*

A Hollerith card is a card used to record information. It has 80 columns and 12 rows. Holes are punched in a particular position on the card to stand for, or represent, data. Hollerith cards are not used by today's computers.

A computer reads a Hollerith card by the position of the holes punched in it.

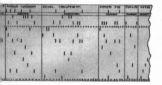

home computer ► **microcomputer**

home key *noun*

The home key is a key on a computer **keyboard**. Pressing the home key either moves the **cursor** to the beginning of a line, to the top of a page or to the top of the file. The home key is sometimes used together with another key.

The home key usually has the word 'home' printed on it.

host *noun*

A host is the computer in a **network** or **on-line** information service that provides information.

She connected the modem and entered her password to access the host.

hot key *noun*

A hot key is a key that has been programmed to carry out a **command**. It is often a short cut that can be used instead of making a series of choices from menus. Pressing the hot key **executes** the command immediately.

He programmed a hot key to start the screen saver.

hot link *noun*

A hot link is when data is transferred from one file to another without the user giving a command. Changes made to one file are automatically made to other files when there is a hot link.

A hot link lets more than one file be updated automatically.

housekeeping *noun*

Housekeeping is taking care of, and organizing, computer files. It includes deleting files no longer needed, making **back up** files, putting files in the proper **directory** and reducing **fragmentation**.

Housekeeping should be carried out regularly.

hybrid computer *noun*

A hybrid computer combines an **analog computer** and a **digital computer**. Hybrid computers are rare. They are sometimes used for weather forecasting.

A hybrid computer uses both analog and digital information.

hypermedia *noun*

Hypermedia is **hypertext** with sound, **graphics** and **video**.

They drove through the solar system using a hypermedia program.

hypertext *noun*
Hypertext is a way of organizing information on a computer. A hypertext file holds groups of information, rather than one page following another. The user can move from one part of the text to another by **clicking** on a special word, or **button**, or on an **icon**.
She clicked on the word rabbit and a page of text came on the screen describing rabbits.

Hz ► hertz

i/o ► input/output

i/o interrupt ► interrupt

icon *noun*
An icon is a small picture that stands for word or group of words. Selecting, or **clicking**, an icon carries out a **comman** Icons make commands easy to recogniz and can be much faster to use than type commands.
She clicked on the icon of a clock to see the time.

if-then-else statement *noun*
An if-then-else statement is used in **programming**. It gives an instruction th something is true THEN carry out the ne instruction ELSE carry out a different instruction.
If-then-else statements can be written o flowchart.

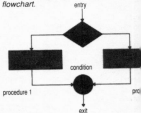

entry

condition

procedure 1

pro

exit

image *noun*
An image is a picture or drawing. It sh how something looks.
An image of a boat was on the screen.

image grabber *noun*

An image grabber, or video catcher, is a device used to get an image, or **frame**, from a video tape or camera and put it into a computer. It is a type of **scanner** that works with software. The user can change, or **edit**, the image using the computer.
An image grabber is very useful for including pictures in desktop publishing.

immediate access store *noun*

The immediate access store is **memory** that the **central processing unit** can use, or **access**, directly.
The immediate access store is also called the main memory.

impact printer *noun*

An impact printer is a **printer** that uses a device to press, or strike, something against a ribbon to put a character on the page.
Line printers, dot matrix printers and daisy wheel printers are all impact printers.

import *verb*

To import is to bring in text or graphics from another program or computer. A special program is sometimes needed to change the **format** of the file being imported so that the two files are **compatible**.
We imported a picture of an elephant.

index *noun*

An index is a list used to find information. An index in a **database** is a list of where to find certain records. An index in programming is a list of where to find data needed by the program.
Most people know how to use the index at the back of a book.

inference engine *noun*

The inference engine is the **software** used by an **expert system**. It is designed to solve a problem in a way that is similar to the way a person would solve the problem.
The inference engine is one of the most important parts of an expert system.

informatics *noun*

Informatics is the combination of **microelectronics** and information. It is the study of how computers handle data.
She decided to study informatics at university.

information retrieval *noun*

Information retrieval is the process of locating information stored on a computer. It usually describes using a computer program to **search** an **on-line database**.
The study of information retrieval also includes the way the information is stored.

information technology (IT) *noun*

Information technology, or IT, is all of the equipment and methods used to handle information. The information is collected, **processed**, stored and used. Modern information technology combines **electronics** and **telecommunications** so that large amounts of data can be stored and **transmitted**.
Televisions, computers, satellites and telephones are just some of the types of equipment used in information technology.

initialize *verb*

To initialize a piece of equipment or a program is to make it ready to use. For example, initializing a program may set all the numbers to zero. To initialize a floppy disk is to **format** it.
The engineer had to initialize the printer.

input device *noun*

An input device is something used to send, or put, information to a computer. There are many different input devices, the most common being a **keyboard** and a **mouse**. **Speech recognition** is being developed to allow a person's voice to input into the computer.

The input device sends data to the central processing unit.

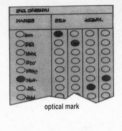

optical mark

magnetic ink

bar code

magnetic stripe

hand-held scanner

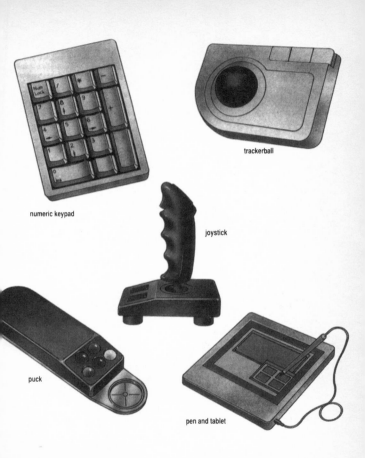

numeric keypad

trackerball

joystick

puck

pen and tablet

ink jet printer   *noun*
An ink jet printer is a type of **printer** that uses sprays, or jets, of ink to form characters on a page. Bubble jet printers are ink jet printers that send drops, or bubbles, of ink in each jet.
An ink jet printer is very quiet.

input   *noun*
Input is the information, or data, entered into a computer. Various types of **input device** are used to enter the information.
A spreadsheet needs input in the form of numbers.

input device ► page 76

input/output (i/o)   *noun*
Input/output is the data going into or out of a device. Input/output can also mean the equipment used to transfer the data.
Input/output is the flow of data through the computer system.

insert   *verb*
To insert is to add something between two other things. For example, a blank line can be inserted between two lines of text.
She inserted the date after her name.

insert key   *noun*
The insert key is a key on a computer **keyboard**. It is a **toggle switch**. When the switch is on, the computer will automatically make space when the user **inserts** text. When the switch is off, new text will replace the text already there.
The insert key is sometimes marked INS.

installation program   *noun*
An installation program is a special program used with a new piece of equipment or software. It helps the user choose the correct settings for the system. The installation program must be run before the equipment or software will work.
Today, most installation programs are user friendly.

instruction   *noun*
An instruction is a line in a **program** that tells a computer what to do. It sends a command to the **processor** to follow certain steps. A computer must have instructions in order to run.
Some computers obey millions of instructions every second.

instruction set   *noun*
An instruction set is the group of all the **instructions** a computer is able to carry out.
Every computer has an instruction set.

integrated circuit ► page 79

integrated services digital network (ISDN)   *noun*
The integrated services digital network is a communications **network** that only uses digital signals. Voice and data can be sent over the same **transmission** line. Most telephone systems are changing from analog networks to digital networks.
A modem is not needed to send data through the integrated services digital network.

integrated software   *noun*
Integrated software is a combination of different types of **applications** programs in the same package. An integrated **spreadsheet**, **wordprocessing** and **database** package allows the user to move data between the applications quickly and easily.
Integrated software is becoming more and more common.

intelligent   *adjective*
Intelligent describes a device which can **process** information. For example, an intelligent terminal has its own processor. An intelligent camera has a **microprocessor** which controls some of its operations.
An intelligent building uses computers to manage the heat, lighting and security services.

integrated circuit *noun*

An integrated circuit is a tiny electronic device that consists of one or more **silicon chips**. Each chip may have thousands of **components** joined together to form **circuits**. They are called 'integrated' circuits because all of the components and the links between them are made as a single piece. Integrated circuits are also known as silicon chips, microchips, or just chips.

Integrated circuits are used for memories and processors in computers and other electronic equipment.

The crystal is sliced into wafers approximately 0.2 mm thick.

Each wafer has hundreds or even thousands of electronic circuits photo-etched on its surface. The wafer is cut into individual chips.

A silicon crystal grown in a laboratory from sand.

Each chip is an integrated circuit. They are mounted on a piece of plastic or ceramic and connected to metal pins. The pins connect the chip to a printed circuit board.

interactive *adjective*
Interactive describes a **program** that asks the user for information or instructions. The program responds to the choices made by the user. An interactive program lets the user choose what to look at or listen to next, instead of simply watching what appears on the screen.
Many multimedia programs are interactive.

inter-block gap *noun*
An inter-block gap is a space between **blocks** of data on a magnetic tape.
The inter-block gap separates different blocks of data.

interface *noun*
An interface is the hardware and software used to let two devices, or a device and a user, communicate. The interface usually follows a set of rules, or a **standard**. It allows devices with different speeds, voltages or codes to work together. For example, an interface allows a **modem** to connect to another modem which uses a different transmission speed. A user interface is designed to stand between a computer program and the user.
Various cables act as interfaces between a computer and its peripherals.

interface processor *noun*
An interface processor is a special **processor** used to handle the flow of information between computers in a **network**.
The interface processor is part of a network.

interference *noun*
Interference is unwanted signals that make it difficult to receive a **transmission**. It can result from natural or man-made causes. Interference can spoil television, telephone, radio and data transmissions.
Interference is sometimes called noise.

interpreter *noun*
An interpreter is a **program** that takes a **statement** in a **high level language** program, translates it and **executes** it. The interpreter then goes to the next statement and follows the same steps.
An interpreter is a type of translator.

interrupt *noun*
An interrupt is a **signal** that stops one job the computer is running so that another job can be carried out. For example, in some wordprocessing programs the user cannot type while an interrupt command is backing up a file automatically.
A message may appear on the visual display unit to explain an interrupt.

inverse video ► **reverse video**

invert *verb*
To invert something is to change it to its opposite. Inverting an image will change each colour to its opposite, or complimentary colour. Black becomes white and white becomes black.
Bit mapped images are easy to invert.

i/o ► **input/output**

ISDN ► **integrated services digital network**

ISO-7 *noun*
ISO-7 is a **character code** used in some computers. It is a seven **bit** code.
ISO-7 stands for International Standards organization seven bit code.

IT ► **information technology**

J

K

joystick *noun*

A joystick is an **input device** that is used to move the **cursor** or other objects on the visual display unit. It is usually used with video games. A button on the top of the joystick sends commands to the computer. Many joysticks also have additional buttons for sending different commands.

When he moved the joystick forward, the man on the screen jumped over the wall.

justification *noun*

Justification is a way of printing or displaying text so that each line begins and ends at the same place. The software inserts the necessary spaces between words to match the length of each line. Text can also be justified to one side or the other. The text in this book is justified left. Most desktop publishing programs can also set the justification to the right.

Justification is an option in most wordprocessing and desktop publishing programs.

justify *verb*

Kbyte ► kilobyte

key *noun*

1. A key is a button on the **keyboard**. When a key is pressed, a signal is sent to the computer. Either a character appears on the visual display unit, or a command is carried out. Different keys can be pressed at the same time to print special characters, or to send commands.

Pressing the enter key moves the cursor to the next line.

2. A key is a special **field** in a **database**. It is the field used to identify the **record**.

The account number was used as the key in the sales database.

keyboard ► page 82

keyword search *noun*

A keyword search is one way, or method, of carrying out a **search** of a **database**. **Full text retrieval** is another method.

A limited number of words can be used in a keyword search.

kilo- *prefix*

Kilo- is used at the beginning of a word to mean one thousand. For example, a kilometre is a thousand metres.

A kilowatt is a thousand watts.

kilobyte (K or Kbyte) *noun*

A kilobyte is a unit of measurement of computer **memory**. A kilobyte is made up of one thousand **bytes**. Computers use **binary code** so a kilobyte is 2^{10}, or 1,024 bytes.

Kilobyte is often abbreviated to Kbyte or K.

keyboard *noun*

A keyboard is an **input device** used to type in information. It has keys for the letters of the alphabet, numbers, symbols and other keys which move the **cursor** around the screen. Many computers also have **function keys**. Striking a key sends a signal to the computer. The signal can be stored on disk, displayed on the screen, and sent to a printer.

Her extended keyboard had function keys and a numeric keypad.

The Qwerty keyboard was designed for manual typewriters. It was designed to slow down typing so that there was enough time for a hammer to reach the ribbon and return without hitting the hammer of the next character.

Various other keyboard layouts have been designed to allow faster typing. This is a Dvorak layout.

When the key for the letter Z is pressed, an electric current sends the code for Z to a microprocessor on the keyboard's circuit board. The code is translated into ASCII code and sent to disk, to the VDU, or to a printer.

One type of keyboard uses keys which have a spring inside them. Other types use a rubber dome.

This keyboard can be adjusted so the user can decide how far apart their hands will be.

This keyboard is designed to be faster and easier to use. The typist's fingers do not need to stretch as far, and their wrists do not need to bend as much.

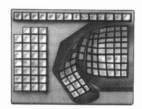

This keyboard is designed to be used by the left hand only.

This keyboard is used along with an ordinary one. It has function keys the user can program, and a built-in trackerball.

kilohertz (kHz)   *noun*
Kilohertz is a unit of measurement of
frequency. It is equal to one thousand
hertz.
*The radio station was broadcasting at 800
kilohertz.*

kilowatt (kW)   *noun*
A kilowatt is one thousand watts. Kilowatts
are used to measure electrical power.
*Large computer systems use many kilowatts
of electrical power.*

kimball tag   *noun*
A kimball tag is a
small piece of
cardboard that has
holes punched in it.
The position of the
holes record
information that can
be read by a special
machine and **input**
into a computer.
Kimball tags are
machine readable.
*Kimball tags help
keep track of the
goods sold in a shop.*

L

label   *noun*
1. In a computer program, a label is a
name, or identifier, given to a **statement**.
*In BASIC, the label for a statement is a line
number.*
2. In a **spreadsheet** program, a label is the
text placed in a **cell**.
The label in cell B5 was 'MAY'.

LAN ► local area network

landscape   *adjective*
Landscape describes a printed page that is
wider than it is long. Not all printers can print
landscape. The opposite of landscape is
portrait.
*Spreadsheets are usually printed in
landscape format.*

language   *noun*
A language is a group of words which can
be used to communicate. Computer
languages are used to write **programs**. The
words must be used according to the set of
rules, or **syntax**, for that language.
*LOGO is a language used to write computer
programs.*

laptop computer   *noun*
A laptop computer is a portable computer
that is small enough to fit in a person's lap.
It can carry out the same tasks as a
microcomputer. The visual display unit is
flat, and usually folds down to become part
of the carrying case. Laptop computers can
use batteries or mains electricity.
*The laptop computer was easy to carry while
travelling between jobs.*

large scale integration (LSI) *noun*
Large scale integration is a way, or
technique, of putting thousands of **circuits**
on one **silicon chip**.
*Large scale integration has been replaced
by very large scale integration.*

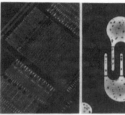

laser *noun*
A laser is a device that sends a very
accurate beam of light. In information
technology, lasers are used to send signals
in **fibre optics**, for reading and writing
optical disks and in some **printers**.
*Laser is the acronym for Light Amplification
by Stimulated Emission of Radiation.*

laser printer *noun*
A laser printer is a **printer** that uses a laser
or other light source to print characters on
the page. The laser puts an electric charge
in the shape of a character onto a rotating
drum. The dry ink, or **toner**, only sticks to
the drum where it has been charged. The
toner is fixed to the paper using heat.
Laser printers are quiet and fast.

layout ► **page layout**

LCD ► **liquid crystal display**

leading *noun*
Leading is the amount of space between
lines of text.
*The amount of leading can be changed by
most desktop publishing programs.*

LED ► **light emitting diode**

letter quality *adjective*
Letter quality describes a printer that prints
sharp, solid characters. Letter quality is also
a setting, or mode, on some types of **dot
matrix printers**. It gives a high **resolution**
of print compared to **draft quality**.
*Letter quality printers are used to print
important letters.*

library *noun*
A library is a collection of **programs** or
routines. These can be used over and over
again. A library may also be a collection of
clip art.
*Programmers can use routines from a library
to save time.*

licence agreement *noun*
A licence agreement is a legal agreement on
how software is allowed to be used. The
agreement is usually printed on the outside
of an envelope containing the disks holding
the software. The user agrees to follow the
conditions of the agreement by opening the
envelope.
*It is illegal to use software without a valid
licence agreement.*

light emitting diode (LED) *noun*
A light emitting diode is an electronic
component that sends, or emits, light when
an electric current is sent to it. Many devices
use light emitting diodes for indicator lights
to show that the power is on, or that the
device is ready to work.
Light emitting diodes are a kind of transistor.

connectors   light emitter

light pen   *noun*

A light pen is an **input device**. There are
two types of light pen. One type is used to
draw on a special screen. The other type of
light pen is used to **read** information from
bar codes. It sends signals to the computer
according to the thickness and spacing of
the black lines it passes over.
A light pen lets the user draw on the
computer screen.

line feed   *noun*

A line feed is the movement of a piece of
paper in a printer. The paper moves up one
line.
Most printers have a button that will send a
line feed command.

line of sight   *adjective*

Line of sight describes a type of
transmission through the air. The signal
travels between two **antennae**. There must
be a clear path between the antenna
sending the signal and the antenna receiving
the signal. Microwave towers use line of
sight transmission.
Obstacles such as buildings or mountains
will block a line of sight transmission.

line printer   *noun*

A line printer is a type of printer. It prints a
complete line of text at a time. Line printers
use a chain or drum with all the characters in
a **character set** on it. The chain or drum
moves and prints the necessary character in
the right place.
A fast line printer can print 2,000 lines a
minute.

liquid crystal display (LCD)   *noun*

A liquid crystal display is a type of screen
used to display information. An electric pulse
causes areas of the screen to change
colour. Laptop computers use liquid crystal
displays because they do not use very much
power.
A liquid crystal display is made up of two
plates of glass with a special liquid in the
middle.

LISP   *noun*

LISP is the **acronym** for LISt Processing.
It is a **high level language** used to write
programs. LISP is often used to write
wordprocessing and desktop publishing
applications and is also used in **artificial
intelligence**.
LISP programs must be translated by an
interpreter.

list   *noun*

A list is a way of organizing information.
The items in the list are set out one below
the other. A computer works with various
types of list.
A queue is a type of list used in computing.

listing   *noun*

A listing is a printout of data or a program.
A program listing is printed in line number
order. Special paper covered in light bands
of colour is often used to make a listing
easier to read.
The program listing was 34 pages long.

literal *noun*

A literal is a value in a program. One example is a group of characters placed between quotation marks. The quotation marks tell the computer that the information should be transmitted as it is, or literally.
The literal 'Help me' was printed on the page as Help me.

load *verb*

To load is to copy data or program instructions into **RAM**. The data can then be used, or the program run.
He loaded the graphics program.

local *adjective*

Local describes things in one place or area. For example, a **local area network** is often in the same building. A local **variable** has a certain value only within one part of a program.
All the computers in the office were connected to a local printer.

local area network (LAN) *noun*

A local area network is a group of computers linked together with **cables**. The computers can share data, programs and printers.
The office had a local area network of five computers.

log off *verb*

To log off is to leave, or **exit**, from a computer program or system. Log off is sometimes called log out.
It is best to log off before switching a computer off.

log on *verb*

To log on is to **access** a computer program or system. Sometimes a **password** needs to be typed in before the user is allowed to log on. In a **multi-user** system, the computer often keeps track of who used which program and for how long. Log on is sometimes called log in.
The user must give a command to log on to a disk drive.

logic *noun*

Logic is a kind, or branch, of mathematics. It is used in computer programs. Logic is used to find out whether a **statement** is true or false.
AND, OR and NOT gates use logic.

LOGO *noun*

LOGO is a **high level language** used for **programming**. It was designed to teach children how to think using **logic**, and to write programs. Students can draw pictures using a **robot** called a **turtle**. The turtle follows the instructions in a program.
LOGO is often used to teach computer science in schools.

lookup table *noun*

A lookup table is a chart, or table, that holds information. It gives a set of different values for a **variable**. For example, a lookup table for the variable 'address' would hold all of the addresses in a database.
Data in a lookup table is quick and easy for the computer to find.

loop *noun*

A loop is a group of **statements** in a program that are organized in a circle, or loop. The instructions in the statement are repeated until a condition is met. A different instruction is then processed.
A do-while loop is often used in programs.

do-while loop

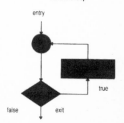

low level language *noun*

A low level language is a programming language that is very close to **machine code**. Each instruction is changed, or translated, into a machine code instruction. Low level languages are translated by an assembler.
Low level languages may be used when speed is important.

lower case *adjective*

Lower case describes the letters of the alphabet when they are written or typed in small letters. Lower case letters are typed without using the **shift key** or **caps lock key**.
All of the letters in this sentence are lower case except for the first one.

LSI ► large scale integration

luggable *noun*

A luggable is a portable computer that is quite heavy or awkward to carry.
The first portable computers were luggable.

M

machine code *noun*

Machine code is a **binary code** that sends instructions to the computer's **processor**. It uses the binary numbers 0 and 1 to tell the computer what to do. Groups of binary numbers are instructions for the computer to **execute**. Programs must be translated into machine code by an **assembler** or a **compiler** before being sent to the processor.
A computer needs instructions in machine code before it can work with them.

machine language *noun*

A machine language is a **programming language** that is very similar to **machine code**. Many of the first programming languages were machine languages.
Machine languages do not need to be translated before the computer processor can work with them.

machine readable *adjective*

Machine readable describes data that can be **input**, using a machine. **Bar codes** and **magnetic ink** are two examples of machine readable data. A **scanner** is used to put the data directly into the computer. Machine readable devices are often used by shops to keep track of the products they sell.
Credit cards carry information as machine readable data stored on the magnetic stripe on the back.

macro- *prefix*

Macro- is a prefix used at the beginning of a word to mean very big.
Something macroscopic is visible to the naked eye.

macro *noun*
A macro is a program instruction that carries out, or executes, a series of instructions. A macro is useful when the same text or a series of commands must be repeated.
The macro named 'Prague' in the wordprocessor typed his address into the file.

magnetic ink *noun*
Magnetic ink is a kind of ink that is magnetic. Characters in magnetic ink can be read by a machine, or are **machine readable**. The machine changes these characters into code so that a computer can work with them.
The numbers along the bottom of most cheques are printed in magnetic ink.

magnetic media *plural noun*
Magnetic media are materials that respond to magnetism. For example, floppy disks are covered in a film containing iron filings. Magnets are used to record information on the disk.
Hard disks, floppy disks and magnetic tape are all examples of magnetic media.

magnetic tape *noun*
Magnetic tape is tape that can record information, or data. **Audio** tape, **video tape**, and computer tape are types of magnetic tape used as **storage devices**.
Magnetic tape comes on a reel, or in a cartridge or cassette.

magneto-optical disk ► **optical disk**

mailshot *noun*
A mailshot refers to a large number of letters or advertisements which are sent out at the same time.
Most wordprocessing programs can be used to do a mailshot.

main logic board *noun*
The main logic board is a **circuit board** inside the computer. It holds **ROM**, **RAM**, a **microprocessor** and other special circuits.
The main logic board is an important part of a computer.

main memory *noun*
Main memory is **memory** used as a temporary storage area for programs and data. It holds the program and data while the program is being used. **Access time** to the main memory is much faster than to a hard or floppy disk. Main memory is RAM, or random access memory.
The instructions that run a software program are loaded into main memory.

mainframe *noun*
A mainframe is a large, powerful computer. Mainframes are mostly used in large organizations. The size and speed of a mainframe is very much greater than that of a **minicomputer**. A mainframe may have hundreds or thousands of **work stations**.
Mainframes process data at a very high speed.

computer tape

data cartridge

record
record
record
inter-block gap

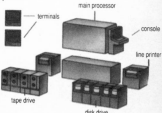

main processor

terminals

console

line printer

tape drive

disk drive

89

maintenance *noun*
Maintenance is keeping something in working order. It includes repairing, testing, adjusting and replacing parts of a computer or a **peripheral**. Maintenance that is carried out after a problem develops is called corrective maintenance. Maintenance carried out before problems develop is preventative maintenance.
Every computer needs a certain amount of maintenance.
maintain *verb*

maintenance contract *noun*
A maintenance contract is a legal agreement with a company. The company agrees to carry out the **maintenance** of equipment in exchange for a fee.
The maintenance contract guaranteed that an engineer would visit the office within 24 hours of a telephone call reporting a fault.

male *adjective*
Male describes a plug that has pins in it. A male plug will connect with a female socket.
Connectors can be described as either male or female.

manual *noun*
A manual is a book that comes with a piece of hardware or software. It explains how to **setup**, **install** and use the machine or program.
The manual for her new software was a 200-page book.

manual *adjective*
Manual describes something done by hand.
Folding letters and putting them into envelopes is a manual job.

mask *noun*
A mask is used when creating a picture, or image. It is used to protect the finished part of the image so that the user can draw around it without damaging it.
A mask is useful when drawing a very detailed picture.
mask *verb*

master file *noun*
A master file is a file which holds important information that does not change very often. It is the main source of information for a user or for another program.
The master file held a list of names and addresses.

master-slave system *noun*
A master-slave system is a **computer system** that uses more than one **processor**. The master computer has the largest, or most powerful, processor. The other computers, or slaves, use the master processor to carry out tasks.
The master-slave system is used in many computer networks.

math coprocessor *noun*
A math coprocessor is an **integrated circuit** designed to carry out mathematical calculations. It is used together with the **central processing unit**. A math coprocessor will speed up processing when a great number of calculations need to be done in a short time.
Many spreadsheet and CAD programs run more quickly with a math coprocessor.

Mbyte ► megabyte

medium *noun*
The medium is the type of material data is stored on. Hard disks, floppy disks and magnetic tape are made of a magnetic medium. Optical disks, punch cards and paper tape are other types of medium.
Video tape is the medium used to store video.

mega- *prefix*

Mega- is a prefix used at the beginning of a word to mean one million.
Mega- is a common prefix in information technology.

megabyte (Mb or Mbyte) *noun*

A megabyte is a unit of measurement for computer **memory**. One megabyte is one million **bytes**. One million in **binary code** is 2^{20}, or 1,048,576 bytes.
Today, most hard disks hold many megabytes of data.

megaflop *noun*

A megaflop is a unit of measurement. It is used to measure how fast a computer can carry out mathematical calculations.
A megaflop is a million **floating point arithmetic** calculations per second.
Megaflops are used to describe mainframes and other powerful computers.

megahertz (MHz) *noun*

Megahertz is a unit of electrical measurement. It measures the **frequency** of a **signal**. One megahertz is one million cycles per second.
A speed of around 25 megahertz is average for minicomputers.

memory ► page 92

memory map *noun*

A memory map is a table that sets out how the storage, or **memory**, of a computer is organized. Memory is given to programs, the visual display unit, and to the keyboard.
A memory map is useful to a systems analyst.

memory resident *adjective*

Memory resident describes programs which are held in the **main memory** all the time. Other programs are only called to the main memory when they are in use.
Parts of the operating system are memory resident.

menu *noun*

A menu is a small list that appears on the visual display unit. It gives the user a choice of commands to carry out. Menus may be in words, or in pictures, or **icons**. There are **pull down**, **pop up** and **pop down menus**.
Menus help the user to move around a software program.

menu-driven *adjective*

Menu-driven describes a software program that uses menus to display **commands**. The commands appear on the screen, and do not have to be memorized.
Menu driven software is user friendly.

merge *verb*

To merge is to bring two different kinds of information, or two or more files, together. For example, mail merge will add the names from an address file onto a form letter. Two files can be merged into one large file.
She had to merge the invitation with the addresses of all her friends in London.

message switching *noun*

Message switching is a method of handling information being sent over a **communications** device. A central computer receives messages from computers in different locations. It stores the messages and then sends, or **transmits**, them to their destination when a **path** is open.
Message switching is used on a network.

91

memory *noun*

Memory is a device where data and programs are stored. Most computers have **integrated circuits** for their **main memory**. These are **ROM** and **RAM** chips. Some computers have a **bubble memory** or a **charge-coupled device**. Computer memory is measured in **bytes**. Another word for memory is storage.

The amount of memory a computer has is an important point to consider when buying a new computer.

A bubble memory device is a tiny, flat wafer, often made out of garnet. It is not an integrated circuit. Instead, magnetic fields shaped like cylinders store data.

ROM and RAM chips are a computer's main, or primary, memory.

A ROM, or read only memory, chip is used for permanent storage. The program or data is fixed when the chip is manufactured, and cannot be changed.

A RAM, or random access memory, chip reads information from disk and stores information input when the computer is in use. Data can be written to, and read from, RAM.

Many computers also have secondary, or auxiliary, memory.

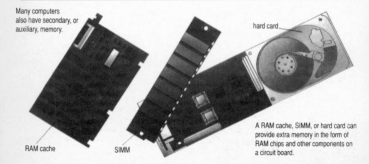

hard card

A RAM cache, SIMM, or hard card can provide extra memory in the form of RAM chips and other components on a circuit board.

RAM cache

SIMM

A hard disk is a magnetic form of RAM. Hard disks retain data even when the computer is switched off. The storage capacity of a hard disk ranges from a few megabytes to over a gigabyte.

Removable hard disks are protected against damage by a hard case. The storage capacity of a removable hard disk ranges from a single megabyte to over a gigabyte.

A Bernoulli disk is a flexible magnetic disk inside a hard, protective case. They are 8 inches or $5\frac{1}{4}$ inches in diameter. The storage capacity of a Bernoulli disk ranges from 10 megabytes to 150 megabytes.

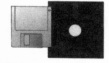

Floppy disks are available in a number of sizes and capacities. There are 8 inch, $5\frac{1}{4}$ inch and $3\frac{1}{2}$ inch diameter disks. The storage capacity of floppy disks ranges from a few hundred kilobytes to four megabytes.

Magnetic tape comes on spools or in cartridges or cassettes. Computer tape has a storage capacity of 1,600 bits per inch or 6,250 bpi. The storage capacity of data cartridges and cassettes ranges from a few kilobytes up to five gigabytes.

Optical storage devices include CD-ROM, WORM, re-writable optical disks and optical cards. The storage capacity of optical disks ranges from 128 megabytes to 1.5 gigabytes.

Memory cards or cartridges are often used with portable computers. Both types are inserted in a special slot in the computer. The storage capacity ranges from a few kilobytes to 20 megabytes.

microcomputer   *noun*

A microcomputer is a small computer often called a personal computer. The most important part of a microcomputer is a **microprocessor**, which is sometimes called its 'brain'. **Peripherals** such as a **keyboard** and **visual display unit** are part of a microcomputer **system**.

A microcomputer is often called a personal computer, or PC.

a typical
microcomputer

visual display unit

drive door lever

5¼" disk drive

3½" disk drive

activity light

disk eject button

numeric keypad

keyboard

mains electricity socket

expansion slots

fan   DIN connector for keyboard   ports

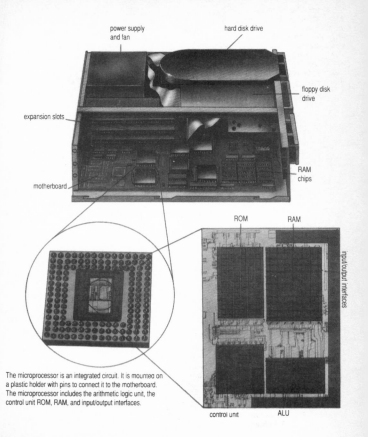

power supply
and fan

hard disk drive

floppy disk
drive

expansion slots

RAM
chips

motherboard

ROM

RAM

input/output interfaces

The microprocessor is an integrated circuit. It is mounted on
a plastic holder with pins to connect it to the motherboard.
The microprocessor includes the arithmetic logic unit, the
control unit ROM, RAM, and input/output interfaces.

control unit

ALU

micro- *prefix*
Micro- is used at the beginning of a word to
mean small.
*Many words to do with computers have the
prefix micro-.*

microcomputer ► page 94

microelectronics *noun*
Microelectronics is a method of working with
very tiny electronic **circuits**. For example,
thousands of circuits can be put on a silicon
chip that is only a few millimetres square.
*Microelectronics must be magnified for
people to see them.*

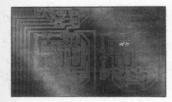

microfiche *noun*
Microfiche is a thin, plastic card with a large
amount of information on it. Photography is
used to record the information on the card.
The text or diagrams have been reduced in
size. A special machine called a microfiche
reader is needed to make the print big
enough for people to read. A card measuring
75 mm × 125 mm holds 48 images.
*One microfiche card can hold many pages
of text.*

microfilm *noun*
Microfilm is a long strip of plastic film, used
to record information. It is similar to
microfiche except the film is in a long roll.
Photographs of documents are recorded on
the microfilm.
*Old newspapers are often put on microfilm
for use in a library.*

microform *noun*
A microform is a document or a group of
documents that have been reduced in size
and stored on film. **Microfilm** and
microfiche are both microforms.
Photography is used to reduce the
documents.
*Using a microform to store paper documents
saves storage space.*

microprocessor *noun*
A microprocessor is a **processor** on a single
silicon chip. It can be **programmed** and it
also contains **memory**. Eight bit
microprocessors have a **word** length of eight
bits. There are also 16 bit and 32 bit
microprocessors which have word lengths of
16 or 32 bits.
*The microprocessor is the central
processing unit in most microcomputers.*

microsecond *noun*
A microsecond is one-millionth of a second.
It is used to measure how long it takes a
processor to carry out instructions.
*Microseconds are used to measure very
short lengths of time.*

microwave transmission *noun*
Microwave transmission is a method of
sending, or **transmitting**, signals. It is used
in **telecommunications** to send radio,
telephone and television signals.
*Microwave transmission works on line of
sight, which means each tower must have a
clear path to the next tower.*

microwave tower — line of sight

MIDI   *noun*

MIDI is the **acronym** for Musical Instrument Digital Interface. It is a set of guidelines, or a **standard**, for connecting **digital** musical instruments to a computer. The user can control the instruments and edit the music using the computer.
The composer used a synthesizer with MIDI to write new songs.

milli-   *prefix*

milli- is used at the beginning of a word to mean one-thousandth.
A milli-second is one-thousandth of a second.

minicomputer   *noun*

A minicomputer is a computer that is more powerful than a **microcomputer**, but not as powerful as a **mainframe**. It is often used by a business where it is not necessary to have a mainframe. A number of **terminals** can be connected to the minicomputer in a **network**.
Ten terminals were connected to the minicomputer at the lumber company's central office.

terminal

minicomputer

MIPS   *noun*

MIPS is the **acronym** for Millions of Instructions Per Second. It is used to measure how many millions of instructions are carried out by a computer's **processor** in one second. MIPS usually measures **machine code** instructions.
A mainframe computer may run at thousands of MIPS.

mnemonic   *noun*

A mnemonic is a shortened word or phrase used to remember something. Mnemonics are often used for commands. For example, 'fmt' is a mnemonic for 'format'. Mnemonics are also useful when naming files. For example, a user might name a file 'letBill' in order to remember that letters sent to Bill are in that file.
Using a mnemonic for a file name makes it easy to remember the contents.

modem   ► page 98

modulation   *noun*

Modulation is a way of changing a **signal**. It changes the **frequency** of the signal. A **modem** uses modulation to put a **digital signal** together with a **carrier signal** so that data can be sent over an **analog** telephone line.
Modulation is often called frequency modulation.

module   *noun*

1. A module is a piece of equipment that is part of a larger system.
A printer is a module in a computer system.
2. A module is part of a **program**. A module performs one task within the program.
Modules are often used when writing very long programs.
modular   *adjective*

monitor   ► visual display unit

mono-   *prefix*

Mono- is used at the beginning of a word to mean one.
A monochrome display can only display one colour.

monochrome   *adjective*

Monochrome describes a **visual display unit** that can only display one colour on the screen.
Monochrome displays are much cheaper than colour displays.

modem *noun*

A modem is a device which lets computers exchange information over telephone lines. The modem changes, or **modulates**, the **digital signal** from the computer into an **analog signal**. When the signal reaches its destination another modem changes the signal back, or demodulates it, from analog to digital code. There are desktop modems, portable modems, and internal modems. *Modem is short for MOdulator/DEModulator.*

digital signal

analog signal

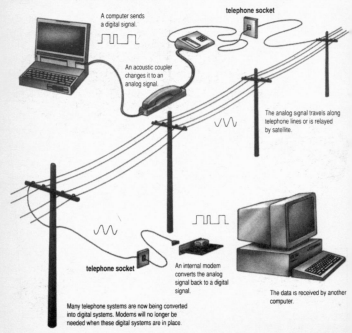

A computer sends a digital signal.

telephone socket

An acoustic coupler changes it to an analog signal.

The analog signal travels along telephone lines or is relayed by satellite.

telephone socket

An internal modem converts the analog signal back to a digital signal.

The data is received by another computer.

Many telephone systems are now being converted into digital systems. Modems will no longer be needed when these digital systems are in place.

mouse (plural **mice**) *noun*
A mouse is a device which is used with
some computers. It is a small plastic box
with buttons on top and a ball underneath.
When the ball is moved over a surface, such
as a desk top, the ball rolls and a marker
appears on the **visual display unit**.
Pressing the buttons on the mouse gives
instructions to the computer.
*He used a mouse to point to the image on
the screen.*

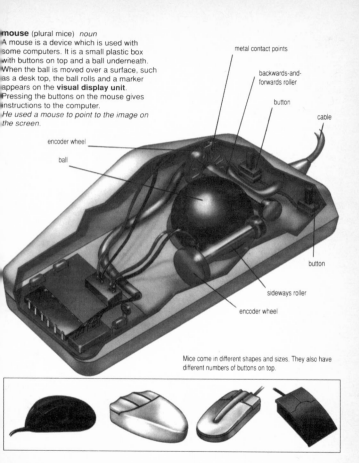

metal contact points

backwards-and-forwards roller

button

cable

encoder wheel

ball

button

sideways roller

encoder wheel

Mice come in different shapes and sizes. They also have
different numbers of buttons on top.

multimedia   *noun*

Multimedia is an **application** that uses
pictures, sound and text. The pictures may
be **graphics**, **animation**, photographs or
video. Multimedia is often **interactive**. It
needs a large **memory**, so **optical disks**
are often used for storage.
*Multimedia is useful in education and in
business.*

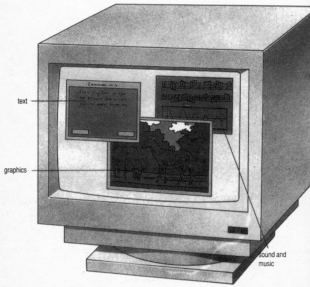

text

graphics

sound and
music

Multimedia software often uses windows to display
information.

Video cameras record moving pictures on videotape.

Special cameras take photographs in digital form.

Speakers let the user listen to sound.

Microphones let the user record sounds and voices.

Musical keyboards can input music.

Special circuit boards are needed for video, sound and graphics.

Optical disks are used for memory.

101

MOS *noun*

MOS is the **acronym** for Metal Oxide Semiconductor. It is a type of **integrated circuit** made in three layers. The first layer is metal. A second layer is oxide. The third layer is a **semiconductor**. MOS technology is used in the manufacture of **large scale integration** chips.
MOS has been replaced by CMOS technology.

motherboard *noun*

The motherboard is the main **printed circuit board** in a small computer. It holds the **central processing unit**, **RAM**, and usually has **expansion slots**.
The motherboard usually sits on the bottom of the computer chassis.

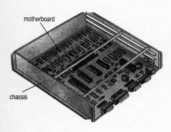

motherboard

chassis

mouse ► page 99

multi-access computer *noun*

A multi-access computer is a computer that many people can use at the same time. Each person works at their own **terminal**. The data is processed by the main computer. Most mainframe and minicomputers are multi-access computers.
The airline had a multi-access computer in its booking office.

multimedia ► page 100

multiplexer *noun*

A multiplexer is a device that takes a number of messages and puts them into a single, high speed **channel** before sending, or **transmitting**, them. A multiplexer is used by **local area networks** that send large amounts of data.
A multiplexer can send a number of different messages at the same time.

multi-tasking *noun*

Multi-tasking is a way of running two or more programs at the same time. It uses **background processing** for one job while the user is working with another program.
Multi-tasking means a user can use a spreadsheet program while the computer finishes calculations for a CAD drawing.

multi-user system *noun*

A multi-user system is a **computer system** that allows more than one person to use, or **access**, programs and data at the same time.
A special version of a software program is often needed for a multi-user system.

musical instrument digital interface ► MIDI

N

name   *noun*
1. A name is a word used in **programming** to identify **instructions**. The programmer only needs to use the name for the instruction to run again.
All of the names in a program are kept in a name table.
2. A name is a word that identifies a file. A name lets the user find the file. Each file must have a different name.
She gave the name 'Pets' to her file about her cat and dog.

NAND gate   *noun*
A NAND gate is a **circuit** that works according to **logic**. When all the inputs are true, the output is false. If any of the inputs are false, the output is true.
A NAND gate is a logic circuit.

nano-   *prefix*
Nano- is used at the beginning of a word to mean one thousand-millionth, or 0.000000001.
A nano-second is one thousand millionth of a second.

natural language   *noun*
Natural language is the language spoken every day by people. English, French and German are natural languages. Some **programming languages** use natural language. It is easier to write programs using natural language than to use special codes or words.
Scientists working in artificial intelligence are developing computers that understand natural language.

near letter quality (NLQ)   *adjective*
Near letter quality describes a printer that can form characters that are better than **draft quality** but not as sharp and clear as letter quality.
Near letter quality printing is done on a dot matrix printer.

nesting   *noun*
Nesting is used in **programming** to place one set of instructions inside another set of instructions. Nesting is often used in **if-then-else** statements.
Writing a program within the main program is called nesting.

network ► page 104

network controller   *noun*
A network controller is a computer that manages, or controls, a **network**. It receives and **transmits** data, sends files to the file server and print server, and acts as a **memory** store.
A network controller is usually a very powerful computer.

networking   *noun*
Networking is working with computers connected in a **network**. It can also describe the job of connecting the computers in the first place.
An expert in networking was called in to design a new network for the office.

nibble   *noun*
A nibble is a unit of measurement for computer **memory**. One nibble is four **bits**, or half a **byte**.
There are four binary digits in a nibble.

103

network *noun*

A network is a group of devices linked together. Information can be passed between the devices. The information usually comes from or passes through a central location. **Telecommunications** networks include television, radio, telephone and computer networks. Computer networks are divided into **local area networks** or LANs, and **wide area networks**, or WANs. *There are six computers in the network.*

Television and radio networks are groups of stations that share programmes or resources.

A telephone network allows telephones, faxes and modems to pass messages between devices connected to the service.

local area networks

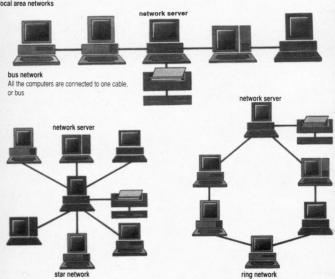

network server

bus network
All the computers are connected to one cable, or bus

network server

network server

star network

Each computer is connected to the network server by a separate cable.

ring network

All the computers are connected to a loop, or ring, of cable.

LQ ► near letter quality

ise *noun*

noise is a sound. In a communications **nsmission**, noise can interfere with the nals being sent. The signal, and the data s carrying, may not be clear when they ch their destination. Noise is a type of **erference**.

ecial communications packages can be ed with computers to check that signals e not affected by noise.

n-volatile memory *noun*

n-volatile memory is **memory** that does t lose its contents when the computer is ned off. Memory in **ROM** is non-volatile mory which is used to store the **erating system**.

hard disk is non-volatile memory found in any microcomputers.

OR gate *noun*

NOR gate is a type of **circuit** that uses gic. It has two or more **inputs** and one **tput**. When both inputs are false, the tput is true. When one or both inputs are e, the output is false.

NOR gate is a logic circuit used in memory d in processors.

OT gate *noun*

NOT gate is a type of **circuit** that uses gic. It has one **input** and one **output**. hen the input is true, the output is false. hen the input is false, the output is true. triangle is used as the symbol for a NOT te.

notebook *noun*

A notebook is a type of portable computer. It can usually be held in one hand, and runs on batteries.

He used a notebook to store his diary.

notepad *noun*

A notepad is a special area of memory. It is used when moving data or graphics from one place or file to another.

A notepad can also be used to display a message to the user.

Num lock key *noun*

The Num lock, or numeric lock, is a key on a computer keyboard. It is a **toggle switch** used to tell the computer to take **input** from the **numeric keypad**.

The cursor cannot be used when the Num lock key has switched the keyboard to the numeric keypad.

number cruncher *noun*

A number cruncher is a powerful computer programmed to carry out a lot of calculations in a very short time.

The physics department needed a number cruncher to process its data.

numeric *adjective*

Numeric describes something that has to do with numbers. Numeric data is made up of numbers rather than letters.

Computers work with numeric data very quickly and accurately.

numeric keypad *noun*

A numeric keypad is a small keyboard that only has numbers on it. It is sometimes built into one side of a computer keyboard. The numeric keypad makes it easier and faster to type in numbers for calculations.

The accountant used the numeric keypad more than the rest of the keyboard.

object oriented programming system
► OOPS

OCR ► optical character recognition

octal system *noun*
The octal system is a number system based on the number eight. It uses the eight digits 0 through 7. Each octal **digit** stands for three **binary** digits. For example, the octal digit 2 stands for the binary code 010.
The octal system is used by some computers instead of the binary system.

off-line *adjective*
Off-line describes a device that does not have a **path** open to the **central processing unit**. It cannot send or receive signals.
A printer is taken off-line when a new ribbon is fitted.

on-line *adjective*
On-line describes a device with a **path** open to the **central processing unit**. Signals can be sent and received by the device.
When a printer is on-line, it is ready to receive data and print.

online database *noun*
An online database is a database available to users in a **network** or over a **modem**. It usually holds information about one subject. For example, the online database may have information on the environment, on a group of businesses, or about books just published.
The online database was updated every day to keep it current.

OOPS *noun*
OOPS is the **acronym** for Object Oriented Programming System. OOPS is a type of programming that groups data with **instructions**. A number of these 'objects' is used in a program.
OOPS is used for hypertext programs.

open *verb*
To open a program is to start it running. To open a file is to display it on the computer's **visual display unit**. Both are opened by typing a command or clicking a **mouse** on an **icon**.
She clicked on the icon of a paintbrush to open the graphics program.

operand *noun*
An operand is a number, or value, used when doing calculations. In the calculation $17 - 9 = 8$, the operands are the numbers 17, 9 and 8. Operands are used in mathematics and **programming**.
In the program instruction ADD C,D, the operands are C and D.

operating system *noun*
The operating system is the main **program** that runs a computer. It controls the use of different parts of the computer, such as **memory**. The operating system also controls the programs and **peripherals** of a computer. It is **loaded** every time the computer is switched on. There are a number of different operating systems, such as **DOS**.
A computer will not work without an operating system.

operation *noun*
An operation is a step, or series of steps, taken to carry out a particular task. For example, delete, add and exit are all operations carried out by a computer. The user gives a **command** to carry out an operation.
She was skilled in the operation of the wordprocessor.

optical character recognition (OCR)
noun

optical character recognition is the ability of a machine to recognize characters. The machine, called a **scanner**, uses light, or optics, to **read** text from a piece of paper. Special software compares the pattern of the signals sent from the scanner to patterns held in **memory**. When a match is made, a signal is sent to the computer.

optical character recognition depends on the computer matching two patterns.

optical disk ► page 108

optical fibre *noun*

optical fibre is a type of **cable**. It is made out of special glass which is stretched into long strands, or fibres. Optical fibre cables are often used to carry telephone signals.
optical fibres carry signals in the form of pulses of light.

optical memory card *noun*

an optical memory card is a small, thin card which has data recorded on it. A laser is used to **write** the data to the card.
an optical memory card can hold over a megabyte of data.

optical storage *noun*

optical storage is any **memory** device that uses light, or optics, to **read** or **write** data.
optical disks such as CD-ROM and WORM disks are types of optical storage.

OR gate *noun*

An OR gate is a type of **circuit** that uses **logic**. It has two or more **inputs** and one **output**. The output of an OR gate is true if any of the inputs are true. If none of the inputs are true, the output is false.
A special symbol is used to represent an OR gate.

input

input

output

output *noun*

1. Output is the result of a **calculation** or **operation**.
The OR gate output was true.
2. Output is information that has been **processed** by a computer. New data is **input**. It goes through the **central processing unit** and is then displayed on the screen or sent to a printer or other **output device**.
Data on a floppy disk is an example of output.

output *verb*

output device *noun*

An output device is a machine that takes information from a computer and prints or displays it. A **visual display unit** and a **printer** are both examples of an output device.
A speaker is an output device used for sound.

overstrike *verb*

To overstrike is to print two characters in the same position. Many **word processing** programs overstrike to put an accent over a letter. The printer will print both characters before moving to the next position on the line.
It is possible to overstrike an S with an I to print the dollar sign.

optical disk *noun*

An optical disk is a thin, circular disk which can store information. Laser light is used to read data from, and write data to, optical disks. Data is stored as either a zero or a one in **binary code**. **Compact disks**, including audio CDs, **CD-ROMs**, CD-I and DVI, are optical disks. **WORM** disks, magneto-optical disks, laser disks and **video disks** are other examples of optical disks. *An optical disk can store much more data than a magnetic disk of the same size.*

an optical disk drive

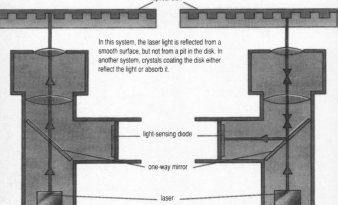

optical disk

In this system, the laser light is reflected from a smooth surface, but not from a pit in the disk. In another system, crystals coating the disk either reflect the light or absorb it.

light-sensing diode

one-way mirror

laser

When the light enters a pit, it is not reflected. The computer reads a 0.

When the light strikes the surface of the disk, it is reflected back to a one-way mirror and then to a light-sensing diode. The computer records a 1.

standard density

double density

quadruple density

Like floppy disks, optical disks have different densities. The higher the density, the more data can be stored on the same size disk.

Laser disks store sound and pictures. They are 30 centimetres, or 12 inches, in diameter. One disk can hold about an hour of video on each side.

Audio CDs store sound only. They are 6, 8, or 12 centimetres in diameter. An 8 centimetre, or $3\frac{1}{4}$ inch, disk holds about 20 minutes of sound. A 12 centimetre, or $5\frac{1}{4}$ inch, disk holds about 75 minutes of sound. CD-ROMs can store sound, pictures and text. They come in 8 centimetre and 12 centimetre sizes. A 12 centimetre CD-ROM can hold about 250,000 pages of text, or up to 650 megabytes.

WORM disks are 12 centimetres in diameter. WORM stands for write once read many. Data can be recorded on these disks only once, and it cannot be deleted. One disk can hold up to 650 megabytes.

Re-writable optical disks are protected by a hard case. They are the only optical disks on which data can be written and erased or deleted. An 8 centimetre disk can hold up to 128 megabytes. A 12 centimetre disk can hold up to 1.5 gigabytes.

overwrite *verb*
To overwrite is to place new data over data already on a storage device. The new data is written over the top of the older data. Overwriting erases the original data.
Many software programs will warn the user if they are about to overwrite a file.

PABX *noun*
PABX is the **acronym** for Private Automatic Branch Exchange. It is a telephone system used by one business or organization inside their building. A PABX can also be connected to the public telephone system for outside calls.
A PABX is used by companies with a large staff.

package ► **software package**

packet switching system *noun*
A packet switching system is a way of sending messages through a **network**. The data to be sent is broken up into small bundles, or packets. The packets are put back together again when they are received by another device.
A packet switching system is used by many computers at the same time.

page break *noun*
A page break is where one page ends and another page begins. It happens automatically in **wordprocessing** when one page is full. A command can be given to put a page break in a certain place.
He split his letter using a page break.

page description language *noun*
A page description language is a **programming language** used to send instructions to a laser printer. It sends information about how a **font** or image should look on the printed page.
A page description language is also used with a typesetting machine.

page layout   *noun*
The page layout is the way a page of text or **graphics** is arranged. It includes line spacing, margins, **fonts** and **justification**.
Desktop publishing programs help the user to be very accurate with a page layout.

page make-up   *noun*
Page make-up describes the job of fitting text and graphics onto a page. It may involve changing the size of a block of text or the size of a picture, so that everything will fit on the page.
Page make-up is done before the final text and graphics are printed.

page printer   *noun*
A page printer is a type of **printer**. It **reads** a page into memory before printing it.
Page printers are faster than line printers.

pages per minute (ppm)   *noun*
Pages per minute is a measurement of the speed of a printer. It measures how many pages the printer can print in one minute.
Many laser printers can print ten pages per minute.

palette   *noun*
A palette is a place for holding paint. In a **graphics** program, it is a kind of **menu** that shows the colours a user can choose. Another palette shows different patterns that can be used to fill a shape.
A palette may include 16 or more colours.

palmtop   *adjective*
Palmtop describes a computer that will fit in the palm of a person's hand.
A palmtop computer will fit into your pocket.

paper tape   *noun*
Paper tape was an early type of **storage device**. Data was recorded by punching holes in various positions on the tape.
Paper tape was used by many early electronic computers.

parallel data transmission   *noun*
Parallel data transmission is a way of sending, or transmitting, data. All of the **bits** that stand for one character are sent at the same time. In an eight-bit computer, eight bits are sent at once.
Parallel data transmission sends eight bits and a parity bit all at the same time.

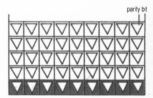

parallel interface   *noun*
A parallel interface is an **interface** that sends and receives a **parallel data transmission**.
A parallel interface is used to connect a computer to a parallel printer.

parallel port   *noun*
A parallel port is a type of **connector**. It is used with a **parallel interface** on devices which use **parallel data transmission**. For example, a parallel printer must be connected to the computer using a parallel **cable** plugged into the parallel port.
Most microcomputers have a parallel port.

parallel processing *noun*
Parallel processing is using more than one **processor** to carry out several different jobs at the same time. Most computers carry out jobs or instructions one at a time.
Only very powerful computers use parallel processing.

parameter *noun*
A parameter is a **variable** used in a **program**. The program looks up the parameter and inserts its value each time the parameter is named.
The value of the parameter named 'year' was 365.

parity bit *noun*
A parity bit is an extra digit, or **bit**, added to each **byte** of data in a **transmission**. The computer checks this bit to make sure that the data has been transmitted correctly. The parity bit causes the sum of all the bits to be either even or odd.
The parity bit tells the computer if a data transmission has been corrupted.

park *verb*
To park a computer is to temporarily lock the **read-write head** in place. This is done to prevent the heads from touching the hard disk, and causing a **head crash**. Some computers park the heads automatically.
Remember to park the hard disk before moving a computer.

parsing *noun*
Parsing is a procedure used by a **compiler** to break down a programming statement into individual instructions.
Parsing is used when translating a high level language.

partition *verb*
To partition is to divide computer **memory** into fixed sections. Each section takes care of a certain program or programs. One section is used for the **operating system**.
Today, it is rare to partition memory.

Pascal *noun*
Pascal is a **high level language** used to write programs. It is used with many microcomputers. Pascal uses **structured programming**.
Several versions of Pascal have been written since the original version of the 1960s.

pass *noun*
1. A pass is one complete cycle of a signal through the **processor**. It includes the **input**, **processing** and **output** of a signal.
Each pass by the computer only takes a fraction of a second.
2. A pass is a complete reading of the **source code** by an **assembler**, **compiler** or **interpreter**.
The compiler made a pass over the program.

passive *adjective*
Passive describes a system which waits for commands from the user.
Most bulletin boards are passive systems.

password *noun*
A password is a secret word a user must type into the computer in order to start a program or open a file. Many software programs require the user to give a password to a particular file. Only other users who know the password are able to open the file.
She gave the password 'Tiger' to her file.

path *noun*
1. A path is the route that a signal takes between two devices. For example, a signal follows a path through an AND gate.
A stream of signals follows a path from the computer to the printer.
2. A path is the route the user must follow to reach a **directory**.
A command to change directories on a hard or floppy disk must include the path.

pattern recognition *noun*
Pattern recognition is a way that a computer can recognize shapes. The computer compares a new shape to the shapes it has stored in **memory**. When a match is found, the computer is said to 'recognize' it. Pattern recognition is used in **optical character recognition**.
The fish processing plant used a computer and pattern recognition to sort the fish as they arrived at the factory.

pay television *noun*
Pay television is a type of television service that is **broadcast** scrambled. It can only be viewed by means of a **decoder**. Some decoders are rented and others are coin-operated.
Many pay television services are broadcast by way of satellite.

PC ► microcomputer

PCB ► printed circuit board

peripheral *noun*
A peripheral is any piece of equipment in a computer system that is not actually inside the computer itself. Computer peripherals include the **keyboard**, **visual display unit**, **printer**, **floppy disks**, **cables** and **manuals**.
A peripheral is controlled by the computer.

floppy disks

trackerball

printer

personal computer ► microcomputer

photoediting ► page 114

pico- *prefix*
Pico- is used at the beginning of a word to mean one million-millionth, or 0.000000000001.
A pico-second is an extremely short period of time.

pin feed ► tractor feed

pirate software *noun*
Pirate software is software that has been copied even though copying is against the law. When software is written, it receives a **copyright**. This means no one can copy the software without permission. **Software houses** try to protect their product from being copied illegally. For example, some software needs a **dongle** before it will work. Other software programs may use a **password** system.
It is not legal to buy pirate software.

photoediting *noun*

Photoediting is working with photographs on a computer. The photograph is changed into digital code by a special **scanner**. The user can then change, or edit, the photograph. The changes can be as small as changing a single **pixel**, or they can change the way the photograph looks entirely.

After photoediting the eye looked as if it was winking.

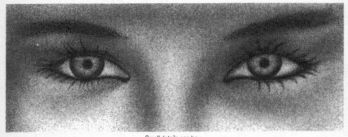

Small details can be
changed pixel by pixel.

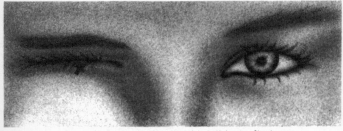

The user can change the colour of a pixel by choosing it with the cursor. Changing
a group of pixels can make a photograph very different from what it was before.

An object in a photograph can be treated as a unit of information. It can be copied and moved. The size and colour can be changed.

Two photographs can be combined to create a picture of something that never happened, or does not exist.

pitch *noun*
Pitch is a measurement used in printing. It is the spacing of characters printed in a certain **font**. The pitch gives the number of characters in one inch. An inch is equal to 25.4 millimetres. The smaller the pitch the closer the characters will be to each other.
The company uses 12 pitch elite for all of their letters.

pixel *noun*
A pixel is the smallest area on a television screen or **visual display unit**. The text or picture on the screen is made up of tiny dots called pixels. The colour and brightness of each pixel is controlled by the computer. A group of pixels form a **bit map**.
Pixel is the short form, or abbreviation, of PICture ELement.

plasma display ► gas plasma display

platen *noun*
The platen is a part of some printers. It is a hard, black rubber cylinder. The paper feeds under and around the platen. The print head strikes the ribbon onto the paper with the platen behind it.
The platen should be kept clean and not marked in any way.

platen

platter *noun*
A platter is one of the disks that make up a **hard disk**. The platters are arranged one above the other on a spindle. Each side of each platter has a **read-write head**.
A hard disk usually has a number of platters.

plotter *noun*
A plotter is a type of printer used to print drawings. Pen plotters are usually **X-Y plotters**. They use a group of different coloured pens that follow instructions about where to start and stop drawing. Other plotters may use **lasers** to put an electric charge on a drum. The ink sticks only where there is an electric charge. **CAD** drawings are output on a plotter.
The map company used a plotter to output their maps.

electrostatic plotter

plug *noun*
A plug is a **male** electrical **connector**. It has pins which fit into the holes in a **female** connector, or socket.
The correct type of plug needs to be used for each piece of equipment.

point *noun*
1. A point is like a decimal point. Computers do not use the decimal system so only the word point is used for this symbol.
Some computers use floating point arithmetic.
2. Point is a unit of measurement for printed characters. It measures the height of a character. There are 72 points in an inch or 25.4 millimetres. **Desktop publishing** programs have different **fonts** which can be printed at different point sizes.
The text in this sentence is printed in 6 point type

point of sale terminal *noun*
A point of sale terminal is a cash register that uses a computer. When a product is sold, information is sent between the cash register and the computer. The information includes the price of the product, and the number of items sold.
Many point of sale terminals use bar code scanners to read the information from the product.

pointer *noun*
1. A pointer is a symbol that shows the user where they are working on the visual display unit. It is a type of **cursor**.
The pointer can be moved around the screen using a mouse or arrow keys.
2. A pointer is used to show where records in a file are kept. The pointer gives the **address** of the record.
The pointer tells the computer where to find a record.

pop down menu ► pull down menu

pop up menu *noun*
A pop up menu is a list of choices, or a **menu**. It is put on the screen wherever the user has positioned the **cursor**. This is useful when the user wants both to read the menu and look at a particular part of the screen at the same time.
A pop up menu can be moved to a different place by moving the cursor.

port *noun*
A port is a connector on the back of a computer or other device. A port is either a **serial port** or a **parallel port** depending on the type of signal being sent. A cable connects the port on one device to the port on another device. For example, a computer is connected to a printer by a cable plugged into a port on the back of the computer at one end and a port on the back of the printer at the other end.
Most computers have more than one port on the back of the machine.

portable computer *noun*
A portable computer is a computer that can easily be carried. It can be powered by batteries or run on mains electricity.
He used his portable computer on the train.

Postscript *noun*
Postscript is a **page description language** used with some laser printers. It can give the printer very accurate instructions about how and where to print text and graphics.
Most desktop publishing programs will work with Postscript.

power surge *noun*
A power surge is a sudden increase in the electricity coming into a machine. This can be caused by a fault in the electrical system, turning on too many machines, or by lightning.
His computer was destroyed by a power surge when lightning hit his house.

ppm ► pages per minute

primary storage ► main memory

print enhancement *noun*
A print enhancement is a change made to the way a **font** looks. Bold, italic and underline are types of print enhancement.
Print enhancement can be used to make words stand out in a document.

printed circuit board ► page 119

printer ► page 120

printout *noun*
A printout is a set of printed pages produced by a printer. It is the **hard copy** of a document held on a computer.
He read the printout of the book report.

priority *noun*
The priority is the importance of one thing compared to another. For example, when many documents must be printed, one document may be more important than the others. It has a high priority and is therefore printed first.
The documents at the bottom of the list have a low priority.

procedure *noun*
A procedure is a sequence of steps taken to carry out a job. In **programming**, a procedure is a number of **statements** in a particular order.
The manual set out the procedure for setting up the printer.

process *verb*
To process is to carry out an action. A computer carries out calculations on data in the form of numbers. It takes **raw data** and processes it to give a result.
A computer is used to process information.
processing *noun*

processor *noun*
A processor is an integrated **circuit**. It is sometimes called the 'brain' of a computer. The processor works with data in the form of electronic signals and sends out the results as new signals. There are many different types of processor, including **microprocessors** and special purpose processors such as **math coprocessors**.
The wordprocessor is often used to mean the central processing unit of a computer.
process *verb*

program *noun*
A program is a complete set of instructions. The instructions are followed by a computer to carry out a particular job. Programs are written in a **programming language**. They are grouped, or classified, as either **application** programs or **systems software**.
She wrote a program which could find out if a number is even or odd.

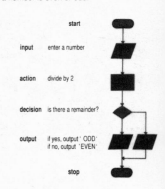

	start	
input	enter a number	
action	divide by 2	
decision	is there a remainder?	
output	if yes, output ' ODD' if no, output 'EVEN'	
	stop	

program generator *noun*
A program generator is a **program** that helps users to write their own programs. It can often take **natural language** and change it into commands which the computer will recognize.
The database package included a program generator.

programmer *noun*
A programmer is a person who writes computer **programs**. Most programmers know a few **programming languages**, but usually only write in one or two of them.
The company hired a programmer to write an accounting program using FORTRAN.

printed circuit board   *noun*

A printed circuit board is a thin, plastic board covered in metal foil. The foil is printed and then etched to form a **circuit**. Various electronic **components** may be mounted on the board. Most electronic devices have a printed circuit board inside them.
The motherboard in a computer is a printed circuit board.

3. The board is etched in an acid bath. The acid eats away the copper except where it is covered by the design.

1. The circuit is designed on a computer.

4. The board is drilled, and the components are mounted and soldered into place.

2. The design is printed onto copper foil by exposing it to ultraviolet light.

5. A typical printed circuit board has a number of different components on it.

printer *noun*

A printer is an **output** device. Data is sent
from the computer to the printer. The printer
puts this data on paper or on special film,
using ink. There are many different types of
printer. The speed of a printer is measured
in **characters per second**, or cps. The
quality of the print is measured in **dots per
inch**, or dpi. Some printers can print in
colour.
*Dot matrix and laser printers are two of the
most common types of printer.*

daisy wheel printer

A daisy wheel has a set of
characters, numbers and
symbols in a particular
typeface. The wheel can
easily be changed for one
with a different typeface.

The daisy wheel spins until the correct letter or symbol is in
the top position. A hammer strikes the letter against a
ribbon, printing the letter on the paper.

dot matrix printer

A series of pins slides in and out of the print head at high
speed. The pins strike a ribbon, and the ink on the ribbon is
transferred to the paper.

Each character is made up of a series of dots printed in this
way.

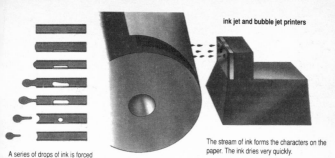

ink jet and bubble jet printers

A series of drops of ink is forced out of tiny holes, or nozzles, at high speed.

The stream of ink forms the characters on the paper. The ink dries very quickly.

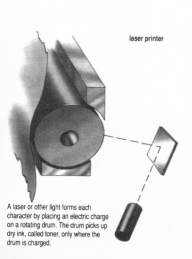

laser printer

A laser or other light forms each character by placing an electric charge on a rotating drum. The drum picks up dry ink, called toner, only where the drum is charged.

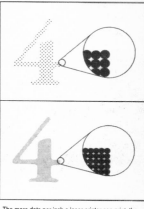

The more dots per inch a laser printer can print, the sharper the character printed on the page.

programming language   *noun*
A programming language is a language made up of special words and symbols. These must be used following the rules, or **syntax**, of the language. Programming languages can be broken down into two main groups, **high level languages** and **low level languages**. There are many different programming languages in use today.
LOGO, BASIC, FORTRAN and C are examples of programming languages.

PROLOG   *noun*
PROLOG is the acronym for PROgramming in LOGic. It is a **high level language** used to write programs. PROLOG is used for **information retrieval** and **expert system** programs.
PROLOG is used to write programs for artificial intelligence applications.

prompt   *noun*
A prompt is a message displayed on the screen to remind the user to do something. The user must type in a reply or a command in response to the prompt. User friendly programs ask the user a question. Some other programs only display a symbol or code.
Many software programs display a prompt to remind the user to save a file before exiting the program.
prompt   *verb*

proportional spacing   *noun*
Proportional spacing is a way of printing text so that the spaces between characters and words look equal. For example, the letter 'i' takes up less space than the letter 'm'. Proportional spacing closes up the extra space around the 'i'. The effect of proportional spacing cannot be shown on most visual display units. Only the printer carries out the command.
Desktop publishing programs use proportional spacing.

protect ► write protect

protected field   *noun*
A protected field is a **field** on a database **record** or a **cell** on a spreadsheet which cannot be changed by the user. It is set by the program or when the file is first used.
The value of a protected field cannot be changed.

protocol   *noun*
A protocol is a set of rules, or a procedure, which is followed when sending data between two devices.
A computer follows a protocol when sending messages to another computer in a network.

prototype   *noun*
A prototype is a working model of a product. It is used to test the design of a product.
The company exhibited a prototype of their new printer.

public domain   *adjective*
Public domain describes software that has no **copyright**. The software is free to be used by anyone. Public domain software is often available on **bulletin boards**.
Shareware is a type of public domain software.

puck   *noun*
A puck is an **input device** used to send information about a printed drawing to the computer. The position of the puck is sent when the user **clicks** a button. A whole drawing may be sent to the computer, or new information can be added to a drawing already on the computer. A puck is often used with a **graphics tablet**.
A puck can be used to enter locations on a map.

pull down menu *noun*

A pull down menu is a **menu** that is
displayed by choosing from a list of menus
at the top of the computer screen. Choosing
a menu causes a list of choices to be
displayed in a column running down from
the top of the screen. An item can then be
selected from this menu by clicking on it with
a **mouse**, or highlighting it with the **cursor**.
*A pull down menu is easy to use with a
mouse.*

pull down menu

punch card *noun*

A punch card is a type of **storage device**
used by older computers. It is a rectangular
card with holes punched in it. The pattern of
the holes represents information. Both
programs and data were stored on punch
cards.
Punch cards are not used any more.

punctuation mark *noun*

A punctuation mark is a special symbol used
when writing sentences. In computing,
punctuation marks can also be used in file
names, and as **wildcard characters** when
carrying out a search.
*Commas, full stops, question marks and
exclamation marks are all punctuation
marks.*

query *noun*

A query is a question. A user types in a
query to request information from a
database.
*The database came up with two choices in
answer to her query for the name of a
computer shop in her neighbourhood.*

query language *noun*

A query language is a special set of words
and commands that is used to **search** a
database. The query language often
includes punctuation marks that can be used
as **wildcard characters**.
*A query language is only used in some
database programs.*

queue *noun*

A queue is a list in a certain order. A printer
lists files in a queue. This shows the order in
which the original print command for each
file was given.
*The file with the earliest print command is
the first file in the queue.*

QWERTY keyboard *noun*

A QWERTY keyboard is a **keyboard** that
has keys arranged in a certain order. It was
designed to keep the speed of a typist slow
enough for the hammer in a manual
typewriter to hit the ribbon and return without
interfering with the next hammer. Most
computers and typewriters use a QWERTY
keyboard. Other arrangements of keys have
been designed, but none of them have
become popular.
*The QWERTY keyboard gets its name from
the first six letters at the top of the keyboard.*

R

RAM *noun*
RAM is the **acronym** for Random Access Memory. It is part of a computer's **main memory**. Data can be read from RAM in any order, or at random. RAM holds the data and programs that are being used by the computer at a given time. Most RAM is volatile, which means the contents are lost when the computer is turned off. Some RAM, called static RAM, or SRAM, will store data even when the computer is turned off.
RAM comes on an integrated circuit.

random access memory ► RAM

raster graphics *noun*
Raster graphics is one way of displaying a picture, or image, on a **visual display unit**. The image is made up of individual dots, or **pixels**. The electron gun in the visual display unit sends a beam of light backwards and forwards across the screen, causing some of the pixels to change colour. The thinnest vertical line is the width of one pixel, so a diagonal line will sometimes look jagged.
Most visual display units use raster graphics.

raw data *noun*
Raw data is the information fed into a computer. It might be a handwritten letter, a list of numbers, or a drawing. The computer **processes** this information to produce reports, spreadsheets, databases or pictures.
It took four hours for the operator to enter the raw data into the computer.

read *verb*
To read data is to move it from a **storage device** into **RAM**. A computer reading a hard disk takes data from the hard disk and moves it into RAM. It can then use the data.
A special machine is needed to read an optical disk.

read only memory ► ROM

READ.ME file *noun*
A READ.ME file is a file included with some software. It gives the user extra information about the program. Usually, this information is too new to be in the **manual**.
A READ.ME file can be read on the screen or printed out.

read-write head *noun*
A read-write head is the device used to **read** and **write** data. It is a part of a **disk drive**. The read-write head sends and receives signals between the disk and the computer.
The read-write head is very close to the disk when reading data.

real time *adjective*
Real time describes an action taken by a computer immediately after receiving data. Information that is put into the computer is acted on, or **processed**, right away. Real time computer systems often use **telecommunications** lines to keep information up to date.
Airlines use real time systems because everyone around the world must know what seats have already been sold on an aeroplane.

record *noun*
A record is one of the **forms** used to keep information in a **database**. For example, a database of names and addresses might hold 100 records. Each record is about one person. **Fields** on the record hold details such as 'city' or 'post code'.
There were over a million records in the database.

recovery program *noun*
A recovery program is a program used to get back data that has been **corrupted** or deleted. Data recovery may or may not work depending on how the data was stored. A recovery program usually works if data was stored on a hard or floppy disk.
The recovery program was able to put the file back together again.

reduced instruction set computer ►
RISC

reformat *verb*
1. To reformat is to **format** a hard or floppy disk that already has data on it. Reformatting puts a new set of **tracks** and **sectors** on a disk. It is carried out if there is an error in reading data from the disk, or if the user no longer needs the data stored on the disk.
When you reformat a disk, all of the data on it is deleted.
2. To reformat in **desktop publishing** or **wordprocessing** is to change the way the page looks.
The page was too crowded, so she decided to reformat it.

refresh *verb*
1. To refresh is to update the display on a television or visual display unit. This is done many times in one second.
The refresh speed must be quite fast or the screen will flicker.
2. To refresh is to regularly send a signal to the computer's **main memory** so that the data remains accurate.
RAM must be refreshed or it will lose data.

register *noun*
A register is a **storage device** in a computer. It is used for special jobs such as arithmetic calculations. The data is stored in the register until the processor is ready for it.
An accumulator is a register.

relational database *noun*
A relational database is a **database** that organizes data in tables. The database can combine information from different tables, and present it to the user.
Most databases are relational databases.

relative address *noun*
A relative address is an area in a computer's memory. It is a number which tells the computer where to find data. The relative address gives the general location of data. It is used to find the **absolute address**.
A relative address is used to find the general area that stores a particular item of data.

remote sensing *noun*
Remote sensing is a method of using **sensors** and **telecommunications** to pick up signals in one location, and send them to a computer in another location. Satellites use remote sensing to send information about planets back to Earth.
Satellites with remote sensing are used to make maps of temperature and vegetation.

rename *verb*
To rename is to change the name of a file or directory. The contents of the file or directory do not change.
He decided to rename his file 'success' after he got an A for his essay.

repeating key *noun*
A repeating key is a key on a **keyboard** that will repeat a character over and over again for as long as the key is held down.
She used the repeating key to put a line of stars underneath her name.

report *noun*
1. A report is a printed document or a verbal speech. It is a summary of an event or a situation.
She wrote a report on the performance of the new computer system.
2. A report is a collection of information taken from a **database** or **spreadsheet** program. The report puts together the information that the user has requested. A report often includes the results of mathematical calculations carried out while the report was being put together by the computer.
The librarian designed a database report to show the total number of books in each subject borrowed from the library last month.

report generator *noun*
A report generator is a special program that helps the user design **reports**. A report generator is used with a **database** program to make it easier to arrange information in a report. The report generator **prompts** the user, and provides on-screen **help**.
Her new database package included a report generator.

reset *verb*
To reset is to cause a computer to **load** the **system software** again after a problem. The computer behaves as if it had been turned off and then on again. The original, or **default**, settings are loaded in an attempt to solve the problem.
Many microcomputers have a special button that will reset the computer when it is pressed.
reset *noun*

resident ► **memory resident**

resolution *noun*
The resolution is the amount of detail that can be shown on a **visual display unit**. The image on the screen is made up of small dots, or **pixels**. The more pixels a screen is made up of, the better the quality of the image on the screen. A high quality screen may be made up of 1,000 pixels. A standard screen may be made up of 200 pixels.
Resolution is measured by the number of pixels on a visual display unit.

retrieve *verb*
To retrieve information is to get, or **read**, it from a storage device. The information can be displayed on the visual display unit.
The user must retrieve a file to be able to look at it.
retrieval *noun*

return key *noun*
The return key is the key on a **keyboard** that is used to move the cursor down to the beginning of a new line. It may also be called the enter key.
She pressed the return key twice to make a new paragraph.

reverse video *verb*
To reverse video is to change the colours on a **visual display unit** to their complementary colours. For example, black is changed to white, and blue is changed to yellow. Reverse video is sometimes called inverse video.
He decided to reverse video the screen to get white letters on a black screen.

ribbon cable *noun*

A ribbon cable is a wide, flat **cable**. It is
made up of rows of wires running side by
·side.

A ribbon cable looks like a ribbon.

ring network *noun*

A ring network is a **network** arranged so
that one cable connects all of the computers
in a complete ring.

*The local area network in our school is a ring
network.*

RISC *noun*

RISC is the **acronym** for Reduced
Instruction Set Computer. It is a computer
that uses a limited number of instructions.

*A RISC processor operates faster because it
has fewer different instructions to work with.*

robot *noun*

A robot is a mechanical device that is
controlled by a computer. Instructions are
sent to the robot to tell it what to do. Modern
robots have **sensors** that pick up and send
signals to the computer. Robots are often
used to carry out jobs which are repeated
over and over again.

*A turtle is a robot used with the
programming language LOGO.*

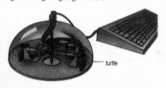

turtle

robotics *noun*

Robotics is the study of how **robots** are built
and how they can be programmed.

*He studied robotics because he was
interested in finding out how machines could
be used to build cars.*

ROM *noun*

ROM is the **acronym** for Read Only
Memory. The data and programs in ROM
can only be **read** by a computer. The
content of ROM is fixed when the ROM chip
or **compact disk** is manufactured. The
content is not lost when the computer is
turned off.

*The user cannot change what is stored in
ROM.*

root directory *noun*

The root directory is the main **directory**. It is
made when a disk is **formatted**. The root
directory contains all of the other directories
and **subdirectories**.

*Systems software is kept in the root
directory.*

routine *noun*

A routine is a set of **instructions** in a
program. The routine carries out one
particular task within the program.

*Some routines are used more than once
in a program.*

row *noun*

A row is a way of arranging data. A row of
data goes across a page or screen. Data in
a **spreadsheet** is arranged in rows and
columns. Each row is given a name or
number. Database **reports** can be arranged
in rows and columns.

The spreadsheet had 34 rows of data.

run *verb*

To run a program is to put it to work on a
computer. A program is running when it is
carrying out **instructions**.

*She decided to run the spell check program
on the file holding her essay.*

run time   *noun*
1. The run time is the length of time that a program is working.
Each student was allowed a run time of 20 minutes to complete the test.
2. The run time is the length of time a program takes to run from beginning to end.
The anti-virus program has a run time of 30 seconds.

S

satellite   *noun*
A satellite is a type of spacecraft. Scientific satellites are launched into space equipped with **sensors** to record information. **Telecommunications** satellites receive and transmit telephone, television and other communications signals. Other satellites are used for **satellite navigation**.
The telecommunications satellite received a signal from Paris and transmitted it to Helsinki.

satellite broadcasting   *noun*
Satellite broadcasting is the **transmission** of television or radio signals by **satellite**. It allows pictures and sound to be broadcast live, or at the time they are happening.
Satellite broadcasting is used to send signals over long distances.

satellite link   *noun*
A satellite link is the use of a satellite to send **telecommunications** signals. The satellite is the link between the station sending the signal and the station receiving it.
Long distance telephone calls often use a satellite link.

satellite navigation   *noun*
Satellite navigation is an electronic system
which uses signals from satellites to locate a
point on or above the Earth. It can be used
to plan and keep track of journeys over land
and sea, and through the air.
Satellite navigation is accurate and reliable.

save   *verb*
To save is to store something in **memory**. A
save **command** must be given. Data can be
recorded on a floppy disk, a hard disk,
magnetic tape, or on another storage device.
*The students were taught to save their work
every 10 minutes.*

scanner ► page 130

scramble   *verb*
To scramble is to take data and mix it up
using a **code**. Data is scrambled so that it
cannot be understood unless the code is
known. This prevents unauthorized people
from understanding the message. The
receiving device uses the code to
unscramble the message.
*The office rule is to scramble all important
documents before sending them over the
modem.*

screen ► **visual display unit**

scroll   *verb*
To scroll is to move quickly through a file on
the **visual display unit**. The file can be
scrolled up or down. The user can move
closer to the beginning or end of the file.
*He pressed the page up key to scroll to the
top of the file.*

scroll bar   *noun*
A scroll bar is a thick line at the side of a
window. The user positions the **cursor**
close to the top or bottom of the bar to tell
the computer to **scroll** closer to the top or
bottom of a file.
*A mouse is often used to position the cursor
on a scroll bar.*

scroll lock key   *noun*
The scroll lock key is a key on some
keyboards. It will send different commands,
depending on the program in use.
*In some programs, pressing the scroll lock
key will stop text from moving up the screen.*

SCSI ► **small computer systems
interface**

search   *verb*
To search is to look for something. A user
can search through a document to find a
word, or **character**. A user can also search
for a **record** in a database, or for a number
of records which have something in
common.
*Doctors can search a medical database for
the most recent information on a drug.*

secondary storage ► **auxiliary
storage**

sector   *noun*
A sector is an area on a hard or floppy disk.
It is a wedge-shaped section. Each sector
has a number of **tracks** running through it.
Data is recorded in **clusters** on one track in
one sector. There are two types of sector,
hard sectors and **soft sectors**.
*The error message told him he had a bad
sector on the hard disk.*

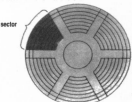

sector

seek time   *noun*
Seek time is the time it takes a **read-write
head** to reach a **track** on a disk.
The disk drive had a fast seek time.

scanner   *noun*

A scanner is an **input device** that transfers information from a piece of paper into a computer. To do this, the scanner sends a beam of light to the page and then measures the amount of light reflected back. White reflects all of the light, black reflects no light, and each colour reflects a different amount of light. The amount of light for each portion is given a **digital code** which is sent to the computer.

Using a scanner is faster than re-typing an entire essay.

flatbed scanner

A document is laid face down on glass. The light moves backwards and forwards.

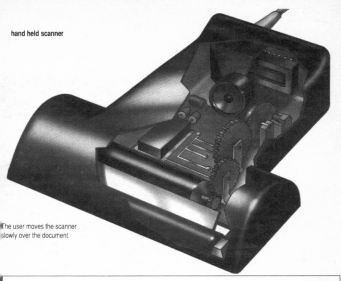

hand held scanner

The user moves the scanner slowly over the document.

Scanners used with optical character recognition software 'look' at printed letters, words, numbers or symbols and try to recognize them from a store of shapes in their memory. If they make a match, they transmit the digital code for the character, often ASCII code, to the computer.

Scanners used to input pictures send digital codes to the computer about colour on a tiny portion of the page. Monochrome scanners register each portion as either black or white. Colour scanners 'look' at the picture three times; once through a green filter, once through a red filter and once through a blue filter.

self test *noun*
A self test is a check that runs automatically.
For example, when a computer is **booted**, a
program tests parts of the **operating
system** to see that they are working
correctly.
*Most printers run a self test every time they
are switched on.*

semantics *noun*
Semantics is the meaning of words or
symbols in a **programming language**. Each
word must have a very precise meaning.
*Computer programmers must know the
semantics of the words they use when
writing a program.*

semiconductor *noun*
A semiconductor is a type of material that
behaves in a certain way. In computers, the
material is silicon. Electricity will not pass
easily through a semiconductor. The word
semiconductor is also used for electronic
components that use semiconductor
technology.
*Transistors, diodes and integrated circuits
are all semiconductors.*

diode

transistor   integrated
                              circuit

sensor *noun*
A sensor is a device that measures
something. There are many different kinds
of sensor. A sensor may measure light, the
distance between objects, or how loud a
sound is.
*Sensors are used on weather satellites to
pick up changes in cloud patterns.*

serial data transmission
noun
Serial data transmission is a
way of sending, or
transmitting, data. Each **bit** of
data is sent one after the other.
The opposite of serial data
transmission is **parallel data
transmission**.
*Serial data transmission is used
by many printers and by most
fax machines and modems.*

serial signals

serial interface *noun*
A serial interface is an **interface** that sends
and receives data one **bit** at a time. It is
often used to link a computer and a
peripheral such as a keyboard or printer.
The RS232 interface is a serial interface.

serial port *noun*
A serial port is a type of **connector**. It is
used with a **serial interface** on devices
which use **serial data transmission**. For
example, a serial printer must be connected
to the computer using a serial **cable** plugged
into the serial port.
Many computers have two serial ports.

serial processing *noun*
Serial processing is used by computers
whose **processor** accepts **bits** of data one
after the other.
*Most computer processors use serial
processing.*

server *noun*
A server is part of a **network**. It is a special
computer that users on the network can
access to carry out a particular job. Users
can share printers, hard disks, and
communications devices such as faxes or
modems.
*Five people wanted to use the printer at the
same time, so the server put the files in a
queue.*

setup *verb*

To setup means to take the necessary steps to get new equipment ready for use. There are usually a number of choices to be made so that the different parts of the **computer system** will work together.

Many programs have a setup command which helps the user input the correct settings for a device.

shareware *noun*

Shareware is a type of **software**. It is a program which is not paid for until the user has tried it and decides to continue using it. Shareware is often distributed over a **bulletin board** or on free disks that come with a magazine. Users are encouraged to share the software.

Shareware is usually cheaper to buy than commercial software.

sheet feeder ► **cut sheet feeder**

shift key *noun*

The shift key is a key on a computer **keyboard**. It is used to tell the computer that a capital, or **upper case**, letter is required. It is also used to choose the symbols which appear above the numbers at the top of the keyboard.

Some programs use the shift key with other keys to give a command.

shielded cable *noun*

A shielded cable is a special type of **cable** used to send data **signals**. It is made up of a **conductor** which **transmits** the signal, and metal wires which surround the conductor to protect it from **interference**.

Coaxial cable is a type of shielded cable.

ship-to-shore *adjective*

Ship-to-shore describes a type of communications system that is used between ships at sea and stations on land. The signals are **broadcast** through the air.

The captain used the ship-to-shore telephone to contact the coast guard station.

signal *noun*

A signal is an electric pulse or wave that carries a message. Computers and telecommunications **devices** send and receive data as signals. The signal may be an **analog signal** or a **digital signal**.

Radio stations broadcast signals through the air.

silicon chip *noun*

1. A silicon chip is a tiny piece of silicon with an **integrated circuit** etched onto it.

Hundreds of silicon chips are cut from each wafer of silicon.

2. Silicon chip is a popular name for **integrated circuit**.

Silicon chips are used for processors and for memory.

SIMM *noun*

SIMM is the **acronym** for Single In-line Memory Module. It is a **circuit board** that holds a number of **RAM** chips. SIMMs are easily added to a computer to give it additional **memory**.

SIMMs are helpful if many programs need to be open at the same time on a computer.

simplex *adjective*

Simplex describes a **transmission** that allows a signal to be sent in one direction only.

A simplex transmission is sent from one device to another.

simulation ► page 134

133

simulation *noun*

A simulation is a model. A computer simulation will respond to the information the user provides. It carries out calculations based on all of the information it has. Results can be predicted for real life situations. A machine built to carry out particular simulation is called a simulator. Simulations are often used for training. For example, flight simulators are used to train pilots.

The research team used a computer simulation to study how an earthquake would affect the bridge.

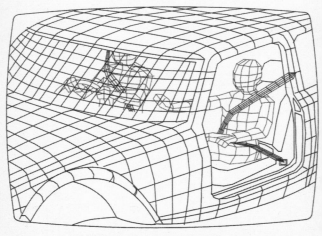

A simulation is often used to study something that would be expensive or dangerous in real life. Motor car crashes and the use of seat belts can be simulated.

Information about the type of motor car, the strength of the materials used to build it, the speed it is travelling, and the people in it are all entered into the computer.

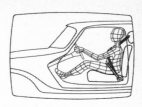

Information about other vehicles and driving conditions can be input. The computer calculates what happens when the motor car is involved in an accident.

The effect of the accident is calculated. The motor car crashes into a tree. The figure is thrown forward but the seat belt stops it from hitting the steering wheel.

single in-line memory module ► SIMM

small computer systems interface (SCSI) *noun*

The small computer systems interface is a set of rules, or a **standard**, for connecting **peripherals** to small computers. For example, hard disks, optical disks and printers can be connected using SCSI.
The small computer systems interface makes it possible for different manufacturers' disks to be used on the same computer.

smart card *noun*

A smart card is a small plastic card that has an **integrated circuit** on it. It can **process**, as well as record, information.
Smart cards are used by telephone companies in some countries.

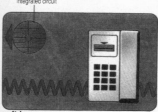
integrated circuit

soft key *noun*

A soft key is a key on a computer **keyboard** that can be used for different things. For example, **function keys** will carry out different commands depending on the software program being used.
The F1 key is a soft key.

soft sector *noun*

A soft sector is an area, or **sector**, of a **floppy disk**. Soft sectors are put, or recorded, on the disk when the disk is **formatted**.
The opposite of a soft sector is a hard sector.

soft space *noun*

A soft space is a space put into a line of text by the software program. It is added to make each line of text the same width. Text is set like this when the **justification** is on.
Desktop publishing and wordprocessing programs use soft spaces to justify text.

software *noun*

Software is the name given to **programs**, **routines** and **procedures** used to operate computer **hardware**. There are three main types of software – **applications** software, **systems software**, and other **tools** used to write these programs.
Most software is supplied on floppy disks.

software house *noun*

A software house is a company or business that writes and develops **software**. Computer scientists, **programmers**, **systems analysts**, engineers, sales people and office staff work for a software house.
Every software house hopes to produce a bestselling software package.

software package *noun*

A software package is a collection, or package, of everything needed to run a **software** program. It includes the software, the user manual, and other documentation. A software package is designed to carry out a particular type of job. It may include more than one **application**.
More than one software program can be included in a software package.

solid modelling *noun*

Solid modelling is a type of computer **graphics**. It is used to make a solid, or three-dimensional, **image** of something. Calculations can be made about the object as if it were a real object. Many CAD programs use solid modelling. The opposite of solid modelling is **wireframe modelling**.
The amount of each material needed to build something can be calculated using solid modelling.

solid state *adjective*
Solid state describes an electronic device
without any moving parts. Electricity causes
changes in solid state devices.
*Vacuum tubes have been replaced by solid
state components.*

mechanical
watch

solid state
watch

sort *verb*
To sort is to organize a group of things into a
particular order. Sorting can put words into
alphabetical order, numbers into numerical
order, or dates into date order. The order
may be **ascending order** or **descending
order**. Sorting is a job computers are very
quick at carrying out.
*The computer was instructed to sort the
names in descending order, so Zachary
came before Yolanda.*

source code *noun*
Source code is code written in a
programming language. It must be
changed into **machine language** by a
compiler or an **interpreter** before the
computer can run it.
*COBOL, FORTRAN and ALGOL are used to
write source code.*

source disk *noun*
The source disk is the disk from which data
is copied. The data is copied from the
source disk onto the destination disk. The
source disk can be a hard or a floppy disk.
*The source disk was the hard disk and the
destination disk was in drive A.*

source language ► **source code**

space bar *noun*
The space bar is a key on a computer
keyboard. It is a long bar at the bottom of
the keyboard. Pressing the space bar inputs
a **hard space**.
*The space bar is used to type a space
between two words.*

specification *noun*
A specification is a description of all of the
equipment needed to carry out a certain
task. It gives details of exactly what will be
required.
*The specification for the computer system
included a fast processor, a laser printer and
two professional graphics programs.*

speech recognition *noun*
Speech recognition is the process of
changing spoken words into code which a
computer will be able to use. A microphone
sends an **analog signal** to a circuit board
which then converts the wave into **binary
code**. The computer compares this code to
codes held as words in the computer's
memory. If a match is made, the computer is
said to 'recognize' the word.
*Scientists are still working on ways to make
speech recognition more efficient and
reliable.*

speech recognition process

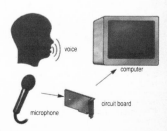

voice

computer

circuit board

microphone

137

speech synthesis *noun*
Speech synthesis is the **output** of noises,
or **audio** signals, that sound like words.
Computers have been developed to use
speech synthesis to read text to blind
people.

spelling checker *noun*
A spelling checker is a program used to
check for words which may have been
spelled incorrectly. The program
compares each word against a dictionary
held in **memory**. If no match is made, the
program displays a list of similarly spelled
words. The user can choose one of these
words to replace the word on the screen.
Most desktop publishing and
wordprocessing programs include a spelling
checker.
The spelling checker asked if she wanted to
replace 'spile' with 'spill'.

spooling *noun*
Spooling is the temporary storage of data
before it is sent on to a slower device. The
data will be sent as soon as the device can
accept it. Spooling allows the user to
continue working on a new or different task.
Spooling is used to send data to a printer,
especially when a number of terminals share
the same printer.

spreadsheet ► page 139

sprite *noun*
A sprite is a picture that a user draws using
a **graphics** program. The sprite can move
around the screen at different speeds and in
different directions.
Her sprite looked like a spider crawling
around on the screen.

SRAM *noun*
SRAM is the acronym for Static RAM. It is
RAM, or random access memory, that does
not lose its contents when the computer is
switched off.
Computer memory cards often use SRAM.

standard *noun*
A standard is a set of rules or g delines.
Standards are written for both **hardware** and
software. They cover areas such as
communications between computers,
connecting **peripherals** to computers, and
how a piece of equipment should operate.
Manufacturers who follow the standards are
able to sell their product for use with any
other device which has also been made
using the same standards.
Standards are important to ensure
compatibility between machines.

star network *noun*
A star network is one type of **network**. All of
the **terminals** in the network are connected
to a special, more powerful computer at the
centre. The terminals are not connected to
each other.
A star network is often used to allow a
number of terminals to use the same printer.

statement *noun*
A statement is a type of instruction given in
programming language. A program is
made up of a number of statements. Each
statement must be translated into **machine**
code before the computer can process it.
If-then-else is a statement used in BASIC.

if<statement>**then**<command>**else**<command2>

if $a=0$ then $b=b+1$ else $a=1$

static memory *noun*
Static memory is memory which does not
lose its contents when the computer is
turned off.
ROM is one type of static memory.

spreadsheet *noun*

A spreadsheet is a table used to calculate the cost of something. Numbers, words and formulae are entered in **cells**. When the contents of a cell are changed, the computer recalculates all the cells affected automatically.

Spreadsheets are often used by a business to come up with a budget.

 A cell can hold a number, or valve.

A cell can hold words, or text.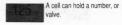

 A cell can hold a formula.

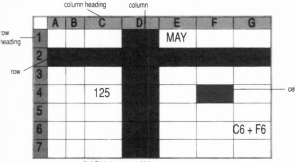

Cell E1 holds the text MAY
Cell C4 holds the number 125
Cell G6 holds the formula C6 + F6

The results of a spreadsheet can be displayed as a graph using business graphics software.

static RAM ► SRAM

still video ► freeze frame video

storage device   *noun*
A storage device is anything which is used to store computer data. **Floppy disks, hard disks, optical disks** and **magnetic tape** are all types of storage device. Storage devices can be internal, such as a hard disk, or removable, such as a floppy disk. They are often called **memory** devices.
She had a 40 megabyte hard disk as her main storage device.

string   *noun*
A string is a group of characters or words. The computer treats the string as one unit. Strings are used in some **programming languages**, such as BASIC. Many programs will also accept a string when **searching** a database or text file.
'Chair' is a string, and so is '2345'.

structured programming   *noun*
Structured programming is a method of **programming**. It breaks down complicated tasks into shorter blocks of work. Structured programming uses these blocks, or **modules**, in a logical order.
Structured programming lets each module be tested independently.

subdirectory   *noun*
A subdirectory is a **directory** within another directory. It is used to keep a group of files separate from a program directory.
He had a subdirectory named 'letters' in his wordprocessing directory.

subroutine   *noun*
A subroutine is a part of a computer **program**. It is a set of instructions to carry out a particular task. The subroutine may be used, or **called**, over and over again in the program.
The program used a number of different subroutines.

supercomputer   *noun*
Supercomputers are the most powerful computers in the world. They can **process** information at extremely high speed.
Supercomputers are often used for weather forecasting.

switch   *noun*
A switch is a device which allows an electric current to be turned off or redirected.
A large telephone exchange may use millions of switches to direct calls to their destinations.
switch   *verb*

synchronous transmission   *noun*
A synchronous transmission is a way of sending, or **transmitting**, data. The data is sent at regular intervals in a continuous stream. The opposite of synchronous transmission is **asynchronous transmission**.
A clock inside the device controls the speed of a synchronous transmission.

syntax   *noun*
Syntax is the correct use of words in a program. A set of rules tells the programmer which words can be used. These words must follow each other in the correct order, or be used in a special way.
The programmer did not put the words in the right order so the syntax was wrong and an error message was displayed.

synthesizer *noun*
A synthesizer is a device that can produce sounds electronically. A music synthesizer imitates the sound of a real musical instrument. A speech synthesizer produces sounds similar to the human voice.
The band used a synthesizer instead of a drummer.
synthesize *verb*

system *noun*
A system is everything needed to carry out a certain task. A computer system includes the **hardware**, **software** and **manuals**. A telephone system includes the telephones, cables, telephone exchanges and satellites used to transmit telephone calls.
Her computer system was expensive because she bought the best of everything.

system crash *noun*
A system crash is when the entire **computer system** stops working. The problem may only be in one piece of software or hardware but nothing in the system will work.
A system crash on a business computer can cause serious problems in the flow of work.

systems analyst *noun*
A systems analyst is a person who is trained to look at how a new computer system will be used, or how an existing one can be improved.
The systems analyst makes sure that the proper programs and hardware are used for the job.

systems disk *noun*
The systems disk is the disk that has the **operating system** and other **systems software** on it. It is needed to start, or **boot**, the computer. When a **microcomputer** has a **hard disk**, it is usually used as the systems disk. A floppy disk can also be used as a systems disk.
Computers without a hard disk must read the systems disk using the floppy drive in order to boot the machine.

systems house *noun*
A systems house is a business or company which designs **computer systems**. It develops **applications** programs and chooses the hardware to run them. Systems analysts and programmers work for a systems house.
A systems house will often install hardware and software for its customers.

systems programmer *noun*
A systems programmer is a person who writes **systems software** for a large computer system.
He was hired as a systems programmer by the bank.

systems software *noun*
Systems software is the software needed to control the running of the computer. Systems software includes the **operating system** and **BIOS**.
A computer needs system software before it can run applications software.

microcomputer + systems software

141

T

tab key   *noun*
The tab key is a key on most **keyboards**.
It moves the cursor across the visual display
unit. The user can set it to move a certain
distance. The tab key is also used to move
between **fields**.
*When he pressed the tab key, the cursor
moved five spaces.*
tab   *verb*

tape drive   *noun*
A tape drive is a device that moves
magnetic tape so that data can be read
from, or written to, the tape. It may be built
into the computer or stand on its own.
*Her computer had a floppy disk drive and a
tape drive.*

tape streamer   *noun*
A tape streamer is a device that uses
magnetic tape to store **back up** files.
*The tape streamer was used to back up the
new files.*

target disk   *noun*
The target disk is the disk onto which a user
copies information. Files are copied from the
source disk to the target disk.
*She copied a file from the hard disk to the
target disk in the floppy disk drive.*

tear-off menu   *noun*
A tear-off menu is part of a menu that can be
moved as a separate piece, or **window**. It
can be placed anywhere on the visual
display unit.
*A tear-off menu makes it easier for the user
to click on an icon.*

technical support   *noun*
Technical support is help given to a
computer user. People who know more
about a software program or a piece of
hardware try to solve any problems the user
is having.
*He called the manufacturer's technical
support department because he could not
understand why the printer did not work.*

telecommunications   ► page 144

teleconferencing   *noun*
Teleconferencing is the use of telephones to
hold a meeting or discussion. It is a service
offered by many telephone companies. More
than two users can take part in the same
telephone conversation. Videoconferencing
is teleconferencing that includes the
tranmission of pictures.
*The company used teleconferencing to hold
a meeting between staff in Tokyo, London
and Paris.*

telepresence   *noun*
Telepresence is the use of a special headset
to send and receive information about a
problem or situation. The person wearing the
headset can send, or **transmit**, pictures and
sound. At the other end, an expert can see
and hear what is happening. Instructions can
be sent back in the form of pictures, text and
sound. The technology for telepresence is
still being developed by scientists.
*A telepresence headset has a camera, a
microphone and speaker, and a small
display screen.*

teletext *noun*
Teletext is an information service. Information is sent, or **transmitted**, at the same time as a television signal. A television set with a **decoder** and a special keypad is needed to use teletext.
Information about the news, weather and entertainment is included in teletext.

television
signal

television set with decoder   database

telex *noun*
Telex is a way of sending written messages. A machine called a teleprinter is used to type in the message to be sent. The message is sent over the telephone system and received by another teleprinter which prints it out.
Telex is less popular now that fax machines are so widespread.

template *noun*
A template is a kind of outline or skeleton of a page or **spreadsheet**. A template has text, graphics, numbers or calculations already on it. The user adds their own information to the template.
He made a template with his name and address to use for all his letters.

tera- *prefix*
Tera- is used at the beginning of a word to stand for the number one million million. It is used in computing to describe the size of storage devices that can hold one million million **bytes**.
A terabyte is so enormous it is difficult to imagine.

terminal *noun*
A terminal is a **visual display unit** and a **keyboard**. It is connected to a separate computer.
A mainframe computer usually has a number of terminals connected to it.

terminator *noun*
A terminator is a symbol used in **programming** and when sending data. The symbol is often a semicolon. The terminator means that an instruction or a message is finished.
The terminator marks the end of a statement.

text *noun*
Text is information, or **data**, in the form of words and numbers. A page of text is full of words rather than pictures or graphics. Text is **input** using a keyboard and a **scanner**.
A wordprocessor is often used to work with text on a computer.

text editor *noun*
A text editor is a **program** that lets the user **input** or change **text**. It is usually a small **utility** program that lets the user change, or **edit**, part of a program. A wordprocessor is a very powerful text editor.
She used a text editor to change a line in her batch file.

text mode *noun*
Text mode is one of the ways, or modes, of displaying text on a **visual display unit**. When the computer is in this mode, it cannot display graphics.
Text mode is only used by some kinds of computer.

thermal printer *noun*
A thermal printer is a printer that uses heat to put characters on the page. It uses paper with a special coating on it. The printer uses heated wires to turn the paper black.
The print quality of a thermal printer is not very good, but the machine is very quiet.

telecommunications *plural noun*
Telecommunications is communication over long distances. Information is moved from one location to another by sending signals through **cables** or through the air. Faxes and computers use the telephone system to send, or **transmit**, and receive messages. *Telephone calls, faxes, television and radio are examples of telecommunications.*

 satellite: receives and transmits telephone, television, radio and remote sensing signals

 cable television: transmits television signals a two-way information services

earth station: transmits and receives telephone, television, radio and remote sensing signals

television broadcasting station: transmits television and teletext signals

microwave tower: receives and transmits telephone, television and radio signals

telephone: transmits and receives signals by way of cable, microwave tower and satellite

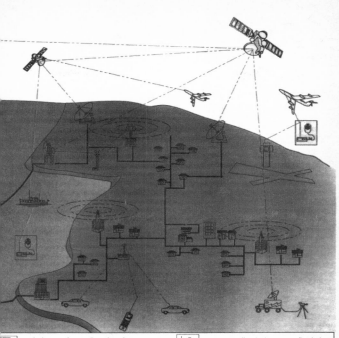

	telephone exchange: directs long-distance calls to a satellite or trunk line cable		**two way radio:** also known as radio telephone transmits calls using radio signals
――――	**cables:** transmit telephone and cable television signals		**cellular telephone:** transmits calls using radio signals, may use cables for long-distance calls
	radio broadcasting station: transmits radio signals		**satellite receiving dish:** receives television and teletext signals

thesaurus   *noun*
A thesaurus is a kind of dictionary in which words are arranged by meaning instead of spelling. It is used to find a word with almost the same meaning as another word. People use a thesaurus when they cannot think of the word they want to use, or to make their writing more interesting.
A thesaurus may be in book or electronic form.

thrashing   *noun*
Thrashing is the condition of a **central processing unit** that is spending more time moving data in and out of **main memory** than it is spending on actually **processing** the data.
Thrashing will slow down a computer processor.

throughput   *noun*
Throughput is a measurement of how much time a **computer system** takes to do a certain job. For example, it may take an hour to print addresses on 1,000 envelopes. A **mainframe** computer in a bank might handle millions of transactions in an hour.
Throughput is important when a job includes lots of calculations.

tile   *verb*
To tile is to place **windows** on the visual display unit so that they do not cover each other. The windows are usually in straight lines. Many software programs using windows have a tile **command**. **Icons** may also be tiled.
She gave the command to tile the windows so she could read what was in each one.

time out   *noun*
Time out is the length of time a computer or other electronic device will wait for a certain signal. If the signal is not received, the device will execute a **command**. The time out is usually set by the manufacturer.
The fax machine has a time out of two minutes.

timesharing   *noun*
Timesharing is a way, or system, of allowing more than one person to use a computer at the same time. A number of **terminals** may all share the same computer. The computer is usually so fast that, although it does one job at a time, the user does not have to wait for results.
Large computers with a number of terminals often use timesharing.

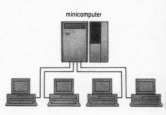
minicomputer

toggle   *noun*
A toggle is a switch or command with only two positions, on and off. The caps lock key is a toggle switch. Pressing it tells the keyboard to send only capital letters to the computer. Pressing it again returns the keyboard to normal, or **default**. Many wordprocessing commands are toggle.
Turning the justification on and off is a toggle in most wordprocessing programs.

token ring network   *noun*
A token ring network is a type of **network**. The computers in the network are connected in a loop, or ring. A message is passed from one computer to the next until it reaches its destination.
A token ring network helps the flow of information in large networks.

toner   *noun*
Toner is a dry powder which is used instead of ink by some printers. The toner is melted, or fused, onto the paper using heat.
Laser printers use toner.

tool *noun*
1. A tool is used in **programming**. It is a program that is used to help write other programs. Tools are also used to find and fix bugs, or **errors**, in a program.
The programmer knew how to use a number of different tools.
2. A tool is something that is used for drawing in a **graphics** program. In many programs, a menu with icons shows the different tools available. If the user chooses the icon of a box, the mouse will draw boxes.
If the paintbrush tool is chosen, lines like those made with a paintbrush can be drawn.

touch screen ► page 148

touch sensitive *adjective*
Touch sensitive describes a keyboard that has no moving parts. The keys only need to be touched, and not pressed down. Touching the key sends an electronic signal.
Many printers and fax machines have touch sensitive controls.

tower *noun*
A tower is a computer that has the case holding the **central processing unit** and the **disk drives** standing up next to the keyboard and visual display unit.
With a tower, the visual display unit sits on the desktop.

trace *verb*
To trace is to look for a mistake, or **bug**, in a **program**. The programmer looks for, or traces, which part of the program contains the bug. It can then be corrected.
A **diagnostic test** may be carried out to trace a bug.
Special programs can be used to help the programmer trace a bug.

track *noun*
A track is an area on a disk or magnetic tape where data is recorded. The tracks on **hard disks** and **floppy disks** are complete circles. The track on an **optical disk** is a spiral. Tracks on magnetic tape may be straight or diagonal.
A $3\frac{1}{2}$-inch floppy disk has 135 tracks per inch.

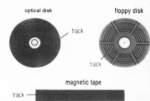

optical disk   floppy disk

track

track

magnetic tape

track

trackerball *noun*
A trackerball is an **input** device used to move the **cursor**. It is a ball which is rotated by the user's fingers. Trackerballs may be on the keyboard, or plug into the computer separately.
A trackerball moves the cursor in the direction the ball is moved.

tractor feed *noun*
A tractor feed is a device attached to some types of printer. It catches hold of **continuous paper** and puts, or feeds, it into the printer. The paper has holes on each side which catch onto pegs on the tractor feed. The pegs turn to move the paper through the printer.
Printers with a tractor feed can be left to print very long documents without attention.

transceiver *noun*
A transceiver is any piece of equipment that can both send, or **transmit**, and receive data.
The word transceiver is made up of the words TRANSmit and reCEIVER.

touch screen *noun*

A touch screen is a computer screen, or **visual display unit**, which responds to the touch of a finger or other pointer. Usually a number of choices is displayed on the screen as pictures, or **icons**. The user touches the icon that represents their choice, and the computer displays information about that choice. The touch screen works by sending a signal to the computer. This gives the location on the screen which has been touched.

Using a touch screen is quick and simple.

A selection of food and drink is displayed. Touching the dessert icon tells the computer to display the dessert menu.

A new screen is displayed, showing icons of the desserts available.

There are different types of touch screen. Some work by breaking, or interrupting, a beam of light or an electric current. Others respond to the pressure of a finger or other pointer. Details of the location are sent to the computer.

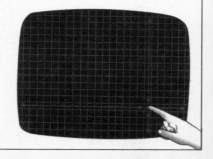

transistor *noun*

A transistor is a **component** used in electronic devices such as computers. They are made from a **semiconductor** material which can act as a two-position switch. Transistors are used to send and store **binary code**. An electric pulse records a 1. No pulse records a 0. Transistors also control logic **gates**, and can make electric signals stronger.
There are tens of thousands of transistors on an integrated circuit.

translator *noun*

A translator is a **program** that can change one **programming language** into another programming language.
A translator is used to change low level language into machine code.

transmission *noun*

A transmission is the data sent from one device to another device. This may be the contents of a fax sent over the telephone system, or a television programme **broadcast** by satellite.
Telecommunications devices transmit and receive different types of **signal** from all over the world.
The radio transmission was broadcast live.

transmit *verb*

To transmit is to send out data or messages. A signal can be transmitted over **cables** or through the air. **Telecommunications** devices often use **satellites** to transmit signals over long distances.
He used a modem to transmit the data to his office in Egypt.

transpose *verb*

To transpose is to change the order of two characters. Transposed letters and numbers are a common typing mistake. For example, if the word 'the' is typed in as 'hte' the user must transpose the 'h' and the 't' to correct the mistake.
She had to transpose 7 and 6 to 67.

transputer *noun*

A transputer is a complete computer on one silicon chip.
Transputers work together in a computer system.

tree *noun*

A tree is a diagram used to show how information is arranged, or how it goes from one place to another. A tree is used in some **operating systems** to show how files are organized in **directories**. A tree is also used to organize a **hierarchical database**, and to show how information is passed from one part of a program to another part.
A family tree is a good example of how information can be arranged in a tree.

tree network *noun*

A tree network is a type of **network**. The computers are arranged along separate lines which are connected to the main cable.
The arrangement of a tree network is similar to the branches of a tree.

troubleshooting *noun*

Troubleshooting is looking for or finding problems in the **hardware** of a computer system. The problem may be quite complicated, or as simple as a loose cable.
A special device called an interfaker is sometimes used for troubleshooting.

troubleshoot *verb*

truncation *noun*
Truncation is making something smaller or shorter. It is used to reduce the number of **digits** so that a number will fit into the allowed storage space. Truncation is also used to make a **character string** shorter.
Using truncation, the string 'computer' was shortened to 'comp'*.
truncate *verb*

trunk line *noun*
A trunk line is a **telecommunications** cable used for long-distance **transmissions**.
A trunk line connects two telephone exchanges.

truth table *noun*
A truth table is used by programmers to write **instructions**. It is used to find out if a statement is true of false. In **binary code** a 1 stands for true, and a 0 stands for false. The program carries out instructions based on this information.
The truth table for an OR gate shows how a 1, or 'true', is output only if one or both inputs are true.

| OR gate truth table | | |
input	input	output
A	B	P
0	0	0
0	1	1
1	0	1
1	1	1

turbo *adjective*
Turbo is a setting for the speed of a **microprocessor**. Some older software runs at a slower speed than new microprocessors.
Many computers have a turbo button which switches the setting.

turtle *noun*
The turtle is the **cursor** used in **LOGO**. A programming instruction might be 'Move turtle left 10'. This moves the turtle ten units across the screen.
A turtle is only used in LOGO.

tutorial *noun*
A tutorial is a program that teaches a person how to use a **software** program. It takes the user step by step through the **menus**, **commands** and other features of the software. A tutorial often gives an example of how the software can be used, with exercises for the student to try.
The tutorial helped her learn the database program.

typeface *noun*
A typeface is a complete **character set** that has a particular design. There are thousands of different typefaces. They each have different shapes, and can be printed at different heights, widths, shapes and thicknesses.
A list of the typefaces in a desktop publishing program is usually found in a font file.

Typeface

Peignot Demi

Typeface

Garamond Bold

typestyle *noun*
The typestyle is the way a **font** or **typeface** is made to look on the screen or on the printed page. The typestyle includes the size, and special features like bold and italic.
The user can change the typestyle by choosing different options on a menu.

U

ultra high frequency (UHF) *noun*
Ultra high frequency is a **transmission** sent at a **frequency** of between 300 and 3,000 **megahertz**.
The radio stations broadcast on ultra high frequency.

UNIX *noun*
UNIX is an **operating system** that can be used with a wide range of computers. It is often used for a **network** or **multi-user** system. UNIX can perform many functions at the same time. It is used by many universities and research centres.
UNIX is used on both microcomputers and mainframes.

update *verb*
To update means to change something so that it includes the latest, or newest information. Updating a file may include adding, deleting or changing information.
When her best friend moved house, she updated her database file of addresses.

upgrade *verb*
To upgrade means to add new or better hardware or software to a computer system.
The school upgraded its computer system to include a laser printer.

upload *verb*
To upload is to send a file to another computer or a **bulletin board**. The file is sent by way of a **modem**, or passed through a **network**.
The computer club decided to upload their latest game to the bulletin board.

upper case *adjective*
Upper case describes capital letters. The first word in a sentence begins with an upper case letter. Pressing the **caps lock** key tells the computer to type and display upper case letters.
Using all upper case letters, the word 'software' becomes 'SOFTWARE'.

user *noun*
A user is the person who works with, or uses, a computer or software program.
The user can decide where to put the picture in a desktop publishing file.

user friendly *adjective*
User friendly describes computer hardware or software that is easy to use. User friendly hardware is simple to set up and run. Software that is user friendly is easy to learn and has a good manual and on-screen **help**.
A reminder to save a file before exiting a program is a user friendly feature of some software.

user group *noun*
A user group is made up of people, or users, who have a shared interest. The members of the group usually all have the same type of computer. A user group may hold meetings, or use a **bulletin board** to exchange information of interest to the members.
A user group is often a good source of information about new equipment.

utility program *noun*
A utility program carries out some of the common tasks needed when using a computer. For example, a utility program copies, or transfers, files to and from a **storage device**. Utility programs, or utilities, are part of the **systems software** of a computer.
Utility programs are usually supplied by the manufacturer of a computer.

video signal *noun*

A video signal is used to send or transmit
moving pictures. It is used to form the
pictures on a television set, **visual display
unit** and video games. A video camera can
be used to record pictures on video tape, or
to broadcast the signal by way of a satellite.
*Video signals are kept separate from sound
signals on video tape.*

video tape

audio   video   control
track   tracks   track

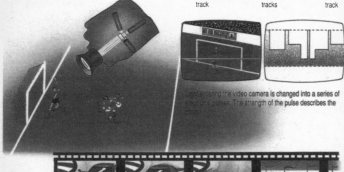

Light entering the video camera is changed into a series of
electronic pulses. The strength of the pulse describes the
colour.

Storing video images on a computer takes up much more
memory than text. One way to overcome this is to record
one frame and then describe, in code, how the picture
changes in the next few frames.

virtual reality   *noun*

Virtual reality is a way of creating a three-dimensional image of an object or scene. It is possible for the user to move through or around the image. Virtual reality imitates the way the real object or scene looks and changes.

Virtual reality is used by some architects to show people what it would be like to walk through a building when it is built.

A data glove is a glove that has sensors which pick up movement. The movements send commands to the computer.

A head-mounted display shows the user the view whichever way they look.

Virtual reality games let the user experience movement and sound while looking at a three-dimensional image.

visual display unit (VDU)   *noun*
A visual display unit is an **output** device
used to show, or display, information from a
computer on a screen. It may be
monochrome or colour. Most visual display
units use a **cathode ray tube**.
*A visual display unit needs a graphics card
to display pictures.*

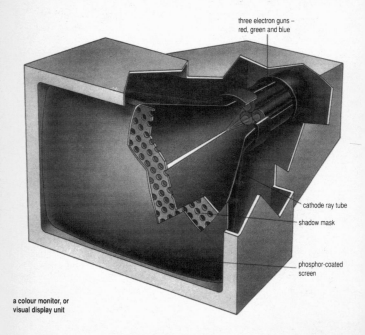

three electron guns –
red, green and blue

cathode ray tube

shadow mask

phosphor-coated
screen

a colour monitor, or
visual display unit

Liquid crystal displays or gas plasma displays are used for portable computers.

Most VDUs use a bit map. The lines and characters are made up of small blocks of colour called pixels.

low resolution text

The more bits, or pixels, per inch, the smoother the image. This is called resolution. A high resolution display is much sharper than a low resolution display.

high resolution text

low resolution graphics

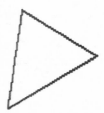

high resolution graphics

vector graphics use lines rather than a bit map

V

value-added network (VAN)   *noun*
A value-added network is a **network** that offers its users special services in addition to the transfer of information. Users of the **network** may receive technical help or have **access** to a database.
Users of a value-added network usually have to pay for the services they use.

variable   *noun*
A variable is something that changes or can be changed. In a computer program, a variable is stored in **memory**. The number or word can change as the program runs.
Each variable is given a name, or reference, so that the computer can find it.

VDU ► visual display unit

vector graphics   *noun*
Vector graphics is a special kind of **graphics** display. The image is made up of lines, rather than **pixels**.
Vector graphics are far more accurate than bit mapped graphics.

version number   *noun*
A version number is a number given to most software programs.
When a program is updated a higher version number is given to it.

very high frequency (VHF)   *noun*
Very high frequency is a **transmission** sent at a frequency of between 30 and 300 **megahertz**.
Some television stations broadcast very high frequency signals.

very large scale integration   *noun*
Very large scale integration, or VLSI, is a method of putting a great number of **components** on a single **silicon chip**. Tens of thousands of components are put together, or integrated, on each chip.
Very large scale integration is used to make integrated circuits.

VGA ► video graphics array

video ► page 152

video graphics array (VGA)   *noun*
Video graphics array is a **standard** for the way information is put on a **visual display unit**. It will only work with some types of computer.
Computers using video graphics array can display a choice of colours.

video tape   *noun*
Video tape is a type of **magnetic tape** that can store moving pictures and sound. It records the picture on **tracks** which cover most of its width. Sound is recorded on a special track along one edge of the tape.
Video tape is used in video cameras and in video cassette recorders.

videoconferencing   *noun*
Videoconferencing is a meeting, or conference, where the users see each other on a screen, and hear each other over the telephone.
Videoconferencing is a new way to hold meetings.

videodisk   *noun*
A videodisk is a type of **optical disk** used to store video pictures and sound. A special machine is used to play, or read, the disk.
A video disk can hold more than 50,000 pictures.

videotex   *noun*
Videotex is a kind of computerized information service. The information is sent out as a television signal. Televisions with the correct **decoder** can **access** the information.
Videotex is arranged in pages of information.

virtual reality ► page 153

virus   *noun*
A virus is a program that has been written to cause problems on someone else's computer. Viruses may cause data to be lost or **corrupted**. A virus is usually passed from computer to computer on floppy disks or over a telephone link.
Special anti-virus software can sometimes be used to stop a virus.

visual display unit ► page 154

VLSI ► **very large scale integration**

voice input ► **speech recognition**

voice messaging   *noun*
Voice messaging is a system of sending and receiving spoken messages over the telephone system. It is a type of **electronic mail**.
Voice messaging is available from telephone companies in many countries.

volatile memory   *noun*
Volatile memory is a type of **memory** that does not store data when the computer is turned off. Another term used for volatile memory is dynamic memory.
The opposite of volatile memory is static memory.

wafer   *noun*
A wafer is a very thin slice of silicon. Hundreds of **silicon chips** are cut from a single wafer.
Wafers are cut from silicon crystals.

white space   *noun*
White space is the area on a printed page that is empty. It is found between paragraphs, and at the top, bottom and sides of a page.
The designer left 25 millimetres of white space for the picture.

wide area network (WAN)   *noun*
A wide area network is a group of computers that communicate over long distances. The computers send data over the telephone system often by way of **satellite**.
The company's wide area network had computers in 30 cities around the world.

wildcard character   *noun*
A wildcard character is used in a **search**. It stands for a character or characters.
A question mark is often used as a wildcard character.

WIMP *noun*
WIMP is the **acronym** for Windows, Icons, Menus, Pointers. The M and P sometimes stand for Mice and Pull down. It is a user **interface** that uses pictures and needs very few typed commands.
WIMP can be used with many programs.

window *noun*
A window is an area on the **visual display unit** that holds information. Many windows can be open, or displayed, at the same time.
Windows can be different sizes, and can overlap each other on the screen.

wireframe modelling *noun*
Wireframe modelling is a type of computer **graphics**. It is used in many **CAD** programs to draw objects using lines and arcs.
No solid surfaces appear on an image drawn using wireframe modelling.

word *noun*
A word is a group of **bits** which a computer stores or retrieves as one unit. Most computers only use one length of word. The length is usually a multiple of eight, which is the number of **bits** used for **character codes**. A 16 bit computer works with a word 16 bits long. There are also 24 and 32 bit computers.
A 24 bit computer stores words of 24 bits.

word wrap *noun*
Word wrap is a feature of **wordprocessing** programs. It automatically sends the cursor to the beginning of the next line when one line is full. Word wrap will also bring text back up a line when words are deleted.
Word wrap is useful because the typist does not need to plan where a line of text will end.

wordprocessing ► page 159

wordprocessor *noun*
1. A wordprocessor is a **dedicated** computer. It is only used for **wordprocessing**.
The office had two wordprocessors.

2. A wordprocessor is a person whose job involves using **wordprocessing** software.
His first job was as a wordprocessor.

WORM *noun*
WORM is the **acronym** for Write Once Read Many. It is a type of **optical disk**. Data can only be **written** to the disk once but can be **read** many times.
A WORM disk holds huge amounts of data.

write *verb*
To write is to record data onto a **floppy disk**, **hard disk** or **magnetic tape**.
A disk drive is used to write data to a disk.

write protect *noun*
Write protect is a way to stop data from being written to a disk or other **storage device**. Floppy disks have a hole or a notch which can be covered up. A light under the disk drive shines up at the hole. If the light passes through, data may be written to the disk. If the hole or notch is covered, data cannot be written to the disk. Computer tape uses a removable plastic ring to write protect.
Write protect keeps data from being deleted.

write enable   write protect

WYSIWYG *noun*
WYSIWYG is the **acronym** for What You See Is What You Get. It is the ability of some software and some **visual display units** to display a page on the screen exactly as it will look when printed on paper.
WYSIWYG is especially useful for desktop publishing.

wordprocessing *noun*

Wordprocessing is working with words on a computer. For example, wordprocessing lets the user type in text, correct mistakes, add or delete text and change the way the words will appear on the page.
Wordprocessing is often used for large numbers of letters.

Text is typed in.

— new line

second paragraph moved to third place

The text can be changed, or edited. The spelling can be checked.

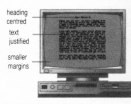

heading centred

text justified

smaller margins

The text can be formatted to change the way it looks on the page.

Sending lots of similar letters is easy. An address file is merged with a form letter.

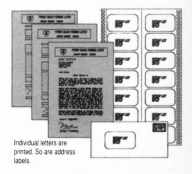

Individual letters are printed. So are address labels.

X

Z

X-on/X-off *noun*

X-on/X-off is the way data is controlled in an **asynchronous transmission**. The computer or device receiving the data sends an X-on **control character** when it is ready to receive data. An X-off control character is sent to stop transmission.

X-on/X-off is a standard used for transmitting data between computers.

x-y plotter *noun*

An x-y plotter is a type of **plotter**. It draws, or plots, a point or line according to a set of numbers. These numbers are locations, or coordinates, on an x-y axis. The x-axis is the horizontal axis. The y-axis is the vertical axis.

An x-y plotter is used for technical drawings.

zero *noun*

Zero is the name for the number 0. A zero in **binary code** stands for off, or false. A zero means no electric current is sent through the circuit.

Zero is one of the two numbers used in binary code.

zoom *verb*

To zoom is to make an image or text larger on the **visual display unit**. This is done to make the picture or words easier to see and work with. The zoom command is usually included in desktop publishing programs and graphics programs. Zoom is also used to make a **window** larger.

She used zoom to increase the size of the dragon's eye until it filled the entire screen.